THE COVER: THE afternoon of September 15th, 1745 and Bonnie Prince Charlie departs Linlithgow Palace on the final stage of his march to Edinburgh.

Front cover illustration by Bill Oliphant

ISBN 0 907 952 003

LINLITHGOW CHURCH & PALACE GATEWAY.

J. Bower fecit

Waldie. Linlithgow.

A HISTORY

OF

THE TOWN AND PALACE

OF

LINLITHGOW

WITH

𝔑𝔬𝔱𝔦𝔠𝔢𝔰, 𝔥𝔦𝔰𝔱𝔬𝔯𝔦𝔠𝔞𝔩 𝔞𝔫𝔡 𝔄𝔫𝔱𝔦𝔮𝔲𝔞𝔯𝔦𝔞𝔫

OF

PLACES OF INTEREST IN THE NEIGHBOURHOOD

BY

GEORGE WALDIE

𝔗𝔥𝔦𝔯𝔡 𝔈𝔡𝔦𝔱𝔦𝔬𝔫

LINLITHGOW:

PRINTED AND PUBLISHED BY G. WALDIE

MDCCCLXXIX

NOTE TO THIRD EDITION.

SINCE the publication of the second edition of this History, our antiquaries have been very busy, and well employed. I have availed myself of their labours to a considerable extent, and my obligations to them will be found acknowledged in the proper places.

LINLITHGOW, *June 1879.*

NOTE TO SECOND EDITION.

IN addition to the acknowledgments in the preface, I have, in this edition, to thank Treasurer PARK for copies of a few interesting documents; and Mr ALEXANDER BROWN for his arrangement of "The rock and wee pickle tow." An Index, and a few notices, which have not before appeared, have also been added, and such corrections made as have appeared requisite.

LINLITHGOW, *March 1868.*

PREFACE TO FIRST EDITION.

IT was originally intended that the following pages should appear as the third edition of a smaller *Sketch of the History of the Town and Palace of Linlithgow*, which, for the convenience of visitors, was published some years ago. The amount of interesting matter, however, contained in the older Burgh records, and in recent publications, to which I have since had access, has enabled me to present a new, and much fuller, and more interesting account than formerly. I had, when preparing the second edition of the above-mentioned Sketch, explored the Council Minutes from 1620 till 1724, and had taken a series of notes, which have served me in good stead now. The older minutes of the proceedings in the Burgh-Court—the open Council of old times—I was not, however, aware of the existence of until they, along with many other documents, were introduced to my notice by W. H. HENDERSON, Esq., who has had occasion, both for literary purposes and for matters connected with Burgh business, to examine the contents of the Charter-chest, and the other records. To his very complete lists of the various documents I have been indebted for much information. To ADAM DAWSON, Esq., Treasurer of the Burgh; and to ROBERT R. GLEN, Esq., Town-Clerk; my thanks are also due for the ready access afforded to the records in their keeping. I have also to thank Mr GEORGE HARDIE, Session-Clerk, for the access afforded to the older minutes of Kirk-Session. To many other friends I am indebted for the use of books, inspection of private papers, and other assistance; to the COUNTY LIBRARY for a perusal of some of the old Acts, and other printed public records, of which it consists; and to the ADVOCATES' LIBRARY for a sight of some of the valuable historical club publications. To Mr GEORGE BROCKLEY I have been indebted for much of what has been preserved traditionally, and for many valuable hints; and to Mr PETER DOW for the excellent Photographs from which the Engravings have been taken, as well as for others of some portions of the old records which defied me to read properly. To Mr SMITH, the present ranger of the Palace grounds, I am also indebted for pointing out some matters connected with the Palace which came under his observation during the recent workings. I have likewise to thank the gentleman who kindly furnished me with the very complete account of the burning of the Covenants. To ARCHIBALD GEIKIE, Esq., of the Government Geological Survey, I am indebted for the very lucid and interesting sketch, which appears in the Appendix, of the Geology of the district: and which, it is to be hoped, is only the prelude to a more extended work.

I had not proceeded very far when I found that the subject had never been subjected to any thorough investigation, and that there was much of error to be cleared away, and much in connection with it that had not, in previous accounts, received due prominence. I do not profess, however, to have exhausted the subject, nor can I hope that more careful examination may not prove me to be in some instances in the wrong.

My attention was caught, at an early stage of the investigation, by one of the papers read at the meeting of the Archæological Institute at Edinburgh, in 1856, by JOSEPH ROBERTSON, Esq., of H.M. General Register House, Edinburgh, by which a considerable amount of light was thrown upon the history of one portion of the Palace; and upon application to him, Mr Robertson not only very kindly consented to the insertion of a portion of the paper, but proffered his assistance in the prosecution of the work. Some of my obligations to him will be found acknowledged in the course of the narrative; and, besides these, I am indebted to him for extracts from the Royal Treasurers' Accounts, and other hints and information not specially noticed.

LINLITHGOW, *May 1858.*

CONTENTS.

CHAPTER I.

CHAPTER II.

CHAPTER III.

CHAPTER IV.

CHAPTER V.

CHAPTER VI.

CHAPTER VII.

CHAPTER VIII.

APPENDIX.

LIST OF ILLUSTRATIONS.

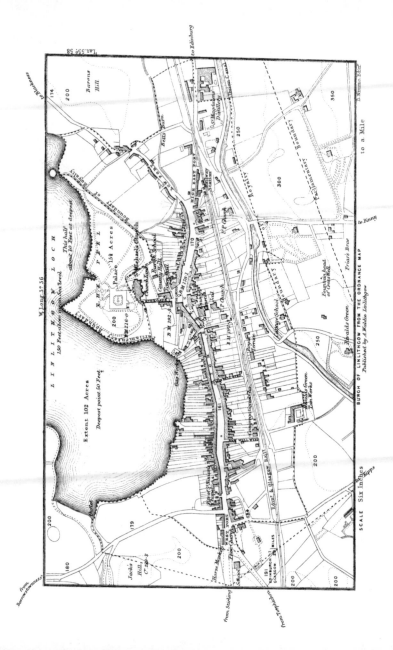

BURGH OF LINLITHGOW FROM THE ORDNANCE MAP
Published by A Waddie Linlithgow

SCALE Six Inches to a Mile

LINLITHGOW LOCH

Extent 102 Acres
Deepest point 50 Feet

150 Feet above the Sea Level

This half about 10 Feet at deepest

Palace

St Michaels Church

Barons Hill

St Magdalene Distillery

Lat 55° 58'

W. Long 3° 36'

to Bo'ness

to Edinburgh

to Binny

to Bathgate

from Bo'ness

from Stirling

from Torphichen

D Newman Edin

Tower, near Railway Station.

CHAPTER I.

INTRODUCTORY AND ARCHITECTURAL.

THERE are few places in Scotland more thoroughly associated with the general history of the country than Linlithgow, lying, as it does, on the road between Edinburgh and Stirling, and on the verge of what has very appropriately been named " Scotland's Battle-field "—that is, the country stretching eastward from Stirling. Its early Castle and subsequent Palace, too, having been a favourite abode of the kings, favoured the growth of the town, which was early endowed with the usual privileges of Royal Burghs, and which rose so far in comparative size and influence as to be substituted in 1368, along with Lanark, in place of Berwick and Roxburgh, as members of the Court of the Four Burghs, so long as these two were held by the English— Edinburgh and Stirling being the other two members. This court, which is still in existence as the Convention of Burghs,

B

had formerly extensive powers, such as the regulation of all
matters of trade not specially provided for by statute, the
apportionment of the taxes contributed by the Burghs, sometimes the farming of the great customs, and generally the
preservation of the rights and privileges of the Burghs
against encroachment.   Linlithgow, although now only forty-
seventh as regards population of the eighty-one Royal and
Parliamentary Burghs of Scotland, long maintained a comparatively forward place.   So late as 1667 it stood ninth in
taxable value, those before it being Edinburgh, taxed £4320
a month, Dundee £840, Aberdeen £800, Glasgow £780, Perth
£480, St. Andrews £326, Kirkcaldy £288, Inverness £264;
Linlithgow was taxed £260, Montrose £240, Haddington
£216, Dumfries £200, and all the others smaller sums.   These
sums are of course scots money, about a twelfth of sterling.
The town is one of the best-preserved specimens of an old
Scotch Burgh we have, and, including the Palace, its remains
of the old times are varied and interesting.

According to Tytler, and other authorities, the houses of the
burgher class were, down to the fifteenth century, invariably
built of wood, and as the town was twice burnt—in 1411 and
1424, the majority of the houses in the town must have been
built since that time.   It may be presumed, however, that the
houses of the greater landowners, as well as the convents,
churches, and public buildings, were of stone.   There are few
of these still existing in the town which have not undergone
some alteration or addition to fit them for the purposes of
subsequent inhabitants.   The most obvious of these alterations is an addition in front, generally with a corbie-stepped
gable-end to the street.   A prominent example, and one of
more architectural pretension than the others, stands on the
west side of the Market-place, and bears the date 1675.   In
the Temple-tenement opposite the Cross, the original stair
remains in front, and enters from the street, a new front
having been added to the old house in a line with the outer
wall of the staircase.   The position of the front stone walls
may be very well seen by examining the gables of the houses,
and the closes.   In all these old houses the under-stories are
solidly arched, and in some instances these are now under-
ground vaults, regarding which there are the usual vague

traditions of subterraneous communications with the Palace. The fronts of some of the houses used to be back from the line of the street. This, in the case of the old houses, arose from the abolition of the wooden "galleries" which used to form the medium of communication between the apartments, and which latterly, when glass became cheap, were, when gable fronts were not added, glazed in front and converted into a second series of apartments. This style of house may be seen perfectly preserved in the present day in the "Rows" of Chester. Sometimes the lower part of the gallery may have been built of stone. An instance of this was brought to light when the plaster was removed from an added gable-front in the centre of the town; and the proprietor, Mr Braes, has very judiciously left open for inspection the mouldings of the arches of what seems to have been an arcade under the upper galleries.

The town lies between the loch and the huge gravel mound on which stand the Palace and Church on the one side, and a steep rising bank on the other, the portion of the street east from and including the Cross being much wider than the longer portion to the west. This mainly arises, no doubt, from there having been more level ground to build upon, although there is some not very certain tradition of there having been a gate at one time at this point dividing the burghal from the royal or aristocratic portion of the town.

It does not appear that there was ever any wall other than that of the "yaird heads," which each proprietor was bound to keep in proper repair, but which, with the "ports" or gates, of which there is now nothing remaining, seems to have been sufficient defence for all ordinary occasions. The town life of the olden time seems to have been somewhat different from that of the present, the burgesses being perhaps as much farmers as tradesmen; one of the old *Leges Burgorum* bears, indeed, that "no man may be Burgess unless he have [in property] a rood of land at the least." Traces of this state of things, fast disappearing, are still to be found in the "acres" or small parcels of land in the neighbourhood of towns, and bearing the names of their former owners; and the following, from a document preserved amongst the town's papers, forms a still more curious memorial of it :—

POINTS OF THE HEAD COURT OF THE BURGH OF LINLITHGOW.

1. { Who Keeps Horses, Cows, or Sheep, and hes not Grass in the Summer nor Provender in the Winter to mentain them, But oppress their Neighbours by Eating their Grass and Corns both night and day.

2.—Who Keeps ffoull Horses.

3.—Who Pulls their Neighbours Stacks.

4. { If it be known that any persons are seen among their neighbours Victuall by Moonlight or other unseasonable hours.

5. { What Children and Prentices are ordinarly amang the Stacks Pulling and destroying the Pease and Breaking the Stackyeard Dykes & Doors.

6. { Who Breaks their Neighbours yeards and Destroys Dovecots or Beehives.

7. { Who deceitfully breaks Bulk of their Coall Loads by the way coming to the Town for their own use or for Sale to others.

8.—Who keeps ffowles that Destroys their neighbours houses and Victuall.

9.—If any are ordinar Swearers, Drunkards, and Nightwalkers.

10.—If any are Guilty of Cutting Young Planting or Destroying Inclosures.

11.—If any hes done Violence to others not Devulged.

12. { If any Person hes Removed March Stones, Land Marks, Breaking Baulks or otherways.

13.—If ye know any Waith Cattle or other Goods, or found or Stoln Gear.

The most remarkable private building in the town is that of which the old square tower near the Railway Station forms a part. It is said to have belonged to the Knights Templars before the suppression of that order, and subsequently to have been the town house of the Knights of St John, or Knights Hospitallers. Very possibly it may have been erected by them after the Wars of Independence, and the decay of the preceptory at Torphichen. There have been two courts surrounded by buildings arched on the ground floor, the courts communicating by an arched way under the square tower, which is again twice arched over internally at different heights. One of the side buildings, with an open oak roof and a fine old fire-place, has possibly been the common hall of these military monks; their chapel has probably been in another part of the building, now destroyed, where a stone coffin containing bones, which crumbled to dust on their exposure to the air, was found some years ago. The building, it is said, was once occupied as a Dominican convent, but the establishment, if it ever existed, seems to have been extinct at the time of the Reformation.

Of the Palace, it is certain that the body of the present erection has been built since the wars of the Edwards. With the exception of the ruined round towers at the north-east, the southern half of the west side seems the most ancient part of the building, but even this is doubtful, there having been so many changes of plan and style. As it stands at present, it forms nearly a square of 168 feet east and west and 174 feet north and south, with a court inside measuring 91 by 88 in the corresponding directions; the heaviness of the mass is relieved on the exterior by battlements, supported by corbels; by additional towers at the corners within the battlements, and by the tops of the four spiral staircases which formed turrets peeping over the roof, and having battlements to which steps ascend outside. The south-east ruined tower is usually called "the Tyler's" [watchman's] tower; and the top of the north-west staircase "Queen Margaret's Bower," from the story that Queen Margaret often sat there watching for the return of King James IV. from Flodden, is a pleasant little octagonal turret, with loopholes looking out in all directions, and a stone seat round the inside, while around the outside a now ruinous open spiral stair led to the summit. The north side of the quadrangle of the Palace—in which is the "foir face" of the following extract from a valuable paper read by the late Mr Joseph Robertson, at a meeting of the Archæological Institute of Great Britain and Ireland, held in Edinburgh in 1856—was rebuilt in 1619–20, as the dates on it bear, and in the style then prevalent, some alterations being at the same time made on the windows of the west side, and furnishes an excellent illustration of the writer's closing remarks. After treating of the Edwardian castles, and of those immediately succeeding, he proceeds :—

Of these oblong towers, one of the earliest and best examples is that of Drum, in Aberdeenshire. Merchiston, in the suburb of this city, and Cawdor and Kilravock, in Nairnshire, are excellent examples of the later style of the second half of the fifteenth century. Borthwick—about ten miles to the south of Edinburgh—is, without question, by far the noblest structure of this class which we possess. It was built a little before the middle of the fifteenth century—an epoch when Scottish architecture, fostered by the love of art which the ill-starred King James III. transmitted to so many of his ill-starred descendants, began to recover from a long season of depression. But its progress was slow, and it is not until near the beginning of the sixteenth century that we can be said to reach a new era. . . . . The chivalrous King

James IV. was, in the latter years of his reign, an energetic builder; but it is not easy always to distinguish between what he built and what was built by his son, King James V. It is important to know from records that both Princes employed continental masons—in the reign of the former, an Italian was at work upon Holyrood; in the reign of the latter, Frenchmen were busy at Stirling, at Falkland, at Holyrood, and at Linlithgow. Of this last edifice —the finest altogether of our Scotch palaces—the larger and better part belongs to the first half of the sixteenth century. What it possesses of foreign aspect is doubtless due, along with the foreign features of Stirling and Falkland, to their foreign builders. In Linlithgow, I may add, the ornamentation partook of the spirit of allegory which runs through the contemporary poetry of Dunbar, Gavin Douglas, and Sir David Lindsay. The now empty niches above the grand gateway in the eastern side of the quadrangle were filled with statues of a pope, to represent the Church; a knight, to indicate the Gentry; and a labouring man, to symbolise the Commons—each having a scroll above his head on which were inscribed a few words of legend, now irretrievably lost. All this I learn from the records of the year 1535, which further show that this group, together with the group of the Salutation of the Virgin upon the other side of the quadrangle, and certain unicorns and a lion upon the outer gateway, were brilliantly painted. The external use of gaudy colour survived in Scotland to a comparatively late date. In the records of the year 1629, for instance, I find a sum of £266, charged for "painting his Maiesties haill rowmes in the Pallice of Linlithgow, both in sylringis [ceilings], wallis, doris, windowis, bordaris above the hingingis; and for furnisching all sortes of cullouris and gold belonging thairto; and lykwayes for painting and laying over with oyle cullour and for gelting [gilding] with gold the haill foir face of the new wark—[that is the north side of the quadrangle built by King James VI.]—with the timber windowis and window brodis, stair wyndowis and crownellis, with ane brod for the kingis armes and houssing gilt and set of; and lykwyse for gelting and laying over with oyle cullour the Four Orderis [that is, the four orders of knighthood held by King James V.] above the vtter yett, and furnisching all sortes of gold, oyle, and warkmanschip thairto, and for laying ouer the two vnicornes and gelting of thame." . . . . . .
The vestiges of brilliant colouring are still perceptible in the crypt of Glasgow; and dim outlines of once resplendent forms are still to be discerned on the walls of the castle halls of Borthwick and Craigmillar. If I give way to the temptation of saying something upon painted glass, it shall be but a sentence or two. In each of the five windows of the chapel in Linlithgow Palace was a figure or image of what the records of 1535 call "made work"—that is, pieced work or mosaic. The price of this was 6s 8d a-foot—the price of the white or common glass being thirteenpence a-foot—both sums, of course, being Scotch money. The five images cost altogether less than £10—the plain glass in which they were set costing £15. The painted glass of the five windows of the Lion Chamber of Linlithgow, executed in the same year, 1535, cost £7— the common glass costing less than £4. To the same age with most part of the quadrangle of Linlithgow, the finest of our Palatial courts, belongs the most part of the quadrangle of Crichton, the finest of our castle courts. Here, again, we meet the marks of foreign taste. . . . I now reach the last, the most prolific, and, as I think, the best age of Scotch secular architecture. King James V. was still busy with his buildings at Holyrood and Linlithgow, at Stirling and Falkland, when the route of Solway broke his heart in 1542. The tumults and wars of the Reformation—extending through the distracted minority, and still more calamitous reign of his hapless daughter—were fatal

to all the arts; and when at length they began to revive under the more peaceful rule of King James VI., about 1570, it was to show how vital a change had been wrought in architectural form and feeling, during an interval of forty years.

To the above it need only be added that the "Lyon Chamber" has been ascertained, from information furnished by Mr Robertson, to be the large hall of the Palace, commonly called the "Parliament Hall" from the circumstance that some meetings of Parliament were held in it. The names of the rooms in these great houses were often given from their principal decorations—thus, according to Mr Robertson, the "court of Troy," in Holyrood, was so called because it was hung with tapestry on which was represented some incidents of the siege of Troy. The Lyon Chamber would in like manner be so called from the emblazonments of arms with which it would be decorated, the principal one being of course the LION of Scotland. One of the vaults below used to be popularly known by the name of "the lion's den"—but whether this was a degenerated tradition of the name of the Lyon Chamber, or whether James IV., who was a wild-beast fancier, actually kept here some part of his collection is not known.

The spirit of allegory which is above alluded to in connection with the statuary of the inner court of the Palace, is farther carried out on the elaborate fountain which adorned it, and again in the Cross Well of the town, an erection originally of about the same date. The other wells for which the town is celebrated in the popular rhyme—

> Glasgow for Bells,
> Lithgow for Wells,
> Falkirk for Beans and Pease—

a rhyme usually wound up by defaming some other town "for Clashes and Lees"—are noways remarkable for their architecture, but two of the oldest bear the heads and names respectively of the Lion Well and the Dog Well, and one of them called after St. Michael, bears his image a-top—one of the statues from one of the older editions of the Cross Well— and has inscribed the date of erection, 1720, with the legend —the origin of which is now unknown—ST MICHAEL IS KINDE TO STRANGERS.

The Church, of which Billings, in his *Baronial and Ecclesiastical Antiquities*, says that it is "assuredly the most important specimen of an ancient parochial church now existing in Scotland, both as to dimensions and real architectural interest," will be more fully treated of in other chapters. The only other old building of any architectural pretension, the Town-house, was originally built in 1668 in an Italian style, with flat roof and ballustrade, and open ballustraded double staircase in front leading to the entrance on the first floor—the jail being beneath. It has undergone many mutations, but still, from the excellence of its original proportions and its prominent position, presents a respectable appearance. The Clock, supplied by public subscription in 1857 to the tower in place of the one which was destroyed in the fire of 1847, was erected by Mr Mackenzie, mechanist, Glasgow, and is the first turret clock constructed in Scotland on the same principles as the celebrated Westminster Palace Clock—the works being principally of cast-iron, and the escapement the new gravity one.

A popular (but incorrect) rendering of the Burgh Arms.

Roman Legionary Tablet found at Bridgeness.

CHAPTER II.

EARLIEST HISTORY AND TOPOGRAPHY.

FOR the times preceding the reign of David I. (1124), the precision of written evidence is very much awanting; but the general features of the history of this district have been pretty clearly made out by our antiquaries from the remains of the works and languages of successive settlers, and from such scanty notices as tradition and cotemporary writings have preserved.

The name of the town and of the county is Celtic. *Lin* means a lake; *lith* or *leith* is half—*leth-aon*, half-one, is a twin in modern Gaelic, and *Ferda-leith* in old Gaelic signified the man or brave of two portions (of the spoil). *Lin-lith* is, then, the lake of two portions—a very accurate description. The *gow* presents the only difficulty. *Ca* or *caw* is still in use in some parts of Scotland for a walk or gang for cattle. *Ca* was once used in a wider sense as synonymous with "district." The district of the double lake is a likely meaning of the word *Linlithgow*. *Cau*, in Welsh, means hollow, shut, or inclosed, so that *Linlithgow* may mean the double lake in the hollow. Many curious etymologies have been given of the name—*Lin* always remaining the same—as *lith*, a twig, and *cu*, a dog, and *liath*, grey, and *cu*, a dog, from Gaelic dialects— etymologies which have apparently been adopted in making up the town's arms—a "greyhound bitch, sable, chained to an oak tree in a loch." This is respectable in comparison with the utter absurdity and childishness of many other heraldic devices. Legends have been attached to the Linlithgow device which are quite as absurd as their origin. Buchanan, in his History, calls Linlithgow *Limnuchum*—probably a Latinised form of a Gaelic name—and in this disguise it appears afterwards in Latin compositions and inscriptions. The old spellings, it may be remarked, almost invariably end with *qw*, and *Linlythqw* is the most prevalent in the times when spelling was very much a matter of fancy; *Linliskeu*, *Linliscoth*, and *Linlychku*, are among the exceptional versions.

The division of the *Lin* or loch must have been even a more conspicuous feature at the time the name was given than it is now, as beds of sedges, and other vegetation, have been found nearly ten feet over the present level, and in one instance, in the eastern part of the town, the paddle of a canoe was got in digging for the foundation of a house; and the remains of a boat were got lately while clearing out the foundation of the new County Court buildings, at the mouth of a small stream which at one time drained into the lake at this place. The loch, indeed, must have covered at one time all the low-lying parts of the town, and may even have stood about forty feet higher than at present, as, excepting the very narrow outlet which the stream has cut through the gravel at the west end, there is no way by which the water could run off below that height; and the Palace mound must have existed in pre-historic times as an island in the middle of an extensive lake.

Of the works of the Celtic tribes in this country, the neighbourhood of Linlithgow affords a now half-ruined Cromlech which stood within a circle of standing stones near the old mansion-house of Kipps, once the property and residence of Sir Robert Sibbald, physician to Charles II., and the only historian the county has found—the *Topographical and Historical Account of Linlithgowshire*, often quoted as *Penney's*, though really forming an excellent county history, being a reprint of the matter contained in *Chalmers' Caledonia*, published in a separate form, with a few additional notes, and a whimsical preface and pseudonyme. On the range of trap hills lying to the south of the town, particularly on Bowden, Cairnpaple, and at Ochiltree-mill, there are fine specimens of what are called Hill-Forts ; and there and at other places stone cists or coffins are now and then disinterred.

That Linlithgow was in these earliest times a town or hamlet, is a traditionary belief, and it has been held that it was the site of a Roman settlement of some sort, and on the first of these points the tradition seems uniform and unchallengeable. The name, *Lindum*, of the Roman geographer, was at one time thought to apply to Linlithgow, but this notion is now abandoned, and no remains of Roman architecture have hitherto been discovered in the immediate neighbourhood— an urn containing 300 coins, however, was, in 1781, turned up by the plough on the Burghmuir, about a mile to the east of the town.

The site of the eastern end of the fortification which the Romans threw across the island from the Forth to the Clyde, lies about four miles to the north of Linlithgow, and a road, once a Roman one, runs along the summit of the hill between, passing on its way the farm-steading now called Walton, but in some old writings Weltoun, from the well, said to be of Roman masonry, still existing there. *Penguaul* was the British name for the head or end of the wall, the Picts changed the *gu* into *f* and called it *Peanfahel,* and the Anglo-Saxons dropped both *gu* and *f,* and adding *tun* for town, called it *penneltun* or *pen-wal-ton.* The present Walton is only the steading of Walton farm, and a mile from and over a ridge and out of sight of the Firth, so is very unlikely to have been the end of the wall. Carriden-house is just about the same distance from Abercorn as Walton, that is, fully three miles of our present measure, which is said to be nearly equal to the two miles of the old monkish writers, one of whom states that the wall commenced at *Caer Eden.* The Roman remains found at and near Carriden-house are thus detailed in the new *Statistical Account* of the Parishes of Scotland (1844) :—

At Carriden various Roman relics have been found at different times, such as a Vespasian of gold ; a stone, described by Gordon as having an eagle with expanded wings, holding a *corona triumphalis* in her bill, and standing in the middle of two Roman *vexilla* or standards, on one side, and on the other the letters COH. IULIA, and others so obliterated as to be illegible, which was built

in a wall added to the house by Alexander Miln, Esq., the then proprietor;
Roman pottery; an old Roman altar, having no inscription, placed at the
time in the garden; and a brass *gladius* or sword, which is now in the Advocates' Library. "About fifty years before" the former Statistical Account
of the parish was written, the author says, that, "in digging up stones to
build a park dyke, axes, pots, and several vases, evidently Roman, were
found, and sent to the Advocates' Library."

Traces of Roman fortification existed in the neighbourhood of
Carriden till the beginning of the present century, and one
place, the site of the ancient wall, still retains the name of
Graham's Dyke. An interesting discovery was made, in April
1868, of a Legionary Tablet, at Bridgeness, in the parish of
Carriden. The Tablet is the largest and finest yet discovered
on the line of the wall, and it is now deposited in the National
Museum of Antiquities in Edinburgh. The slab is of free-
stone, 9 feet long, 2 feet 11 inches broad, and about 9 inches
thick, with holes cut into the edges at the back for fastening
it into a building. At one end, in relief, is a victorious Roman
riding over dead and wounded Britons; and at the other
representatives of the Second Legion offering up sacrifice.
The inscription, literally translated, reads—[Dedicated] To
THE EMPEROR CÆSAR TITUS ÆLIUS HADRIANUS ANTONINUS
AUGUSTUS PIUS, [P.P. for Pater Patriæ] FATHER OF HIS
COUNTRY. LEGION II., THE AUGUSTAN, [per] THROUGHOUT
[M.P. for Millia-Passuum, miles, or] THOUSAND-PACES FOUR
[and] DCLII [paces—4652 in whole of the wall] MADE. The
Roman pace of two steps was 4·84 feet, so that the whole was
4 miles 465 yards, the distance to the Avon. The Tablet
belongs to the wall of A.D. 139. A quantity of squared stones
were found along with the Tablet, but the exact nature of the
building of which they formed part has not been ascertained.
Some of the stones have been built up by Mr Cadell, of
Grange, the proprietor, as a framework for a facsimile of the
inscription, erected at the spot where the Tablet was found.
Blackness is exactly or nearly two of our present miles distant
from Abercorn, and some remains of a causeway running from
Blackness were dug up about fifty years ago on the ridge
above Walton. Blackness has even been supposed to have
been the veritable *Caer Eden.* The finding of the Tablet at
Bridgeness most likely fixes the site of the exact end of the
wall, but not of all the establishments connected with it, as

these, from the nature of the finds at Carriden-house, evidently extended so far, and as *Caer* means wall, fort, or city, the word *Caer-y-din* may mean the city-fort or castle, situated of course at the *pen* or end of the *guaul* or wall. Kinneil has also been supposed to have been the end of the wall, it having been mentioned as *Cenail*, by mistake apparently for *penfahel* by an old writer (*additions to Nennius*). The word has been thought to mean "head of the wall," that is, *Ceann*, head, and *fhail*, of the turf, or fence; but it is more likely to be a corruption of *Kil-Naile*, the church of St. Neill. It is possible, though, that the first line of forts erected under Agricola, about A.D. 81, may have come no farther. The west end of Borrowstounness is called *Corbiehall*, a possible corruption of *Caerfahel*, the fort on the wall. Here and at Inveravon would be two of the small square forts or stations which were distributed between the larger ones, at distances of about two miles along the wall.

Under the Roman occupation, this district seems to have been inhabited by Cymric tribes, speaking a language akin more to Welsh than to Gaelic, and they are usually called the Ancient Britons. The people to the north on the east side of Scotland went by the name of Picts, while those on the west, intimately connected with the north of Ireland, like the Irish, were called Scots. Some Pictish tribes also held the country about what are now called the Pentland hills. After the withdrawal of the Roman legions, the Britons were subject to continual harassment by both Picts and Scots, and by the Saxons, as the rovers from the north of Europe were called. A league of the British tribes was at length formed, and under their pen-dragon, as their commander-in-chief was called, they made considerable head against their enemies. "King Arthur," as one of the principal of the pen-dragons has been called, fought twelve famous battles in which they were victorious. One of these, the battle of Badon, Mr F. W. Skene in his *Four Ancient Books of Wales* is inclined to place near Linlithgow, at the hill of Bowden, already referred to in connection with the old hill-forts. This battle or siege, or relief of the siege —"obsessio Badonici montes" is the entry in the *Chronicle of the Picts and Scots*—took place about the year A.D. 516. According to an old Chronicle, Arthur was slain at the battle of Camlan in 537. Camlan has been supposed to be Camelon, near Falkirk. A second battle of Badon is recorded in 665.

About this time flourished the so-called Welsh Poets, Llewarch-hen, Taliessin, and Aneurin. The great Poem of Aneurin, the *Gododin*, celebrates or laments the fate of his race and country, whose last hopes of independence were extinguished in the great fight at the Catraeth, A.D. 596. Linlithgow was in the country of Gododin, and, according to Mr Skene, bordering on the district called Catraeth, which stretched along the south side of the Firth of Forth to somewhere about Falkirk. The site of this battle has not been satisfactorily settled, but according to Mr Beale Poste, in his *Britannia Antiqua*, it must have been at Carriden, three miles to the north of Linlithgow, where the Roman wall ended, and in the trench and forts immediately to the westward. Viscount Villemarque in his *Les Bardes Bretons*, even thinks he has found an old name of Linlithgow in the poem in his *Lec'hleiku*, to the valiant men of which district the poem makes some reference; *Bodgat*, another name, has been thought to be Bathgate. Mr Skene inclines to place this battle or week's fighting near the Carron.

Sir Robert Sibbald says that there was a tradition of a battle on the hill to the north of Linlithgow loch, between the natives and the Romans. Mr Skene thinks he finds this battle in one of the poems of Taliessin. It is there called " a battle in Agathes in defence," and "a battle of trembling in Aeron. A battle in Arddunion and Aeron." *Aeron* he thinks is the Avon, not far off, and the name *Iron-gath*, which is now applied to some lands on the hillside, a combination of Aeron and Agathes. Iron-gath used to be taken for *Arncath*, the high or hill battle. The battle of the poem, however, would not be between the Romans and the natives, as the Britons called themselves Romans after the departure of the legions. There seems to have been a sort of foray—the poem talks "of kings who were extinguished in the war. Men with full intent to obtain cattle." A place on the hillside has got the name of Swordiemains from the old swords found in the ground about, but none of them seem to have been preserved, else the character of the weapons might have told something.

The district after this was under Saxon domination, although the northern Picts were sometimes in possession, and it was the scene of frequent strife between the Scots and the Picts. Under the Saxon occupation, the usual Romish ecclesiastical system was introduced, a Bishopric and a Monastery having been founded at Abercorn, about five miles from Linlithgow. It had to be abandoned, however, in the end of the seventh century, in consequence of the unsettled state of this border land. Nothing remains of the monastery except a sculptured shaft of a stone cross, now built into the wall of the Abercorn church. A rude and mutilated statue found at St. Ninian's Chapel, Blackness, and now in the Castle, may also belong to the same period.

One rather important battle between the Picts and the Scots seems to have occurred near Carribber, about three miles west from Linlithgow, after this abandonment of Abercorn. It is noted in the *Ulster Annals*, as "Bellum Cnuicc Coirpre i Calathros uc etar linn du." Mr Skene, in his *Celtic Scotland*, gives the following account of the battle :—

A formidable attack was made by Aengus, the Pictish king, upon Dalriada, [the south-west Highlands and north-east corner of Ireland were so called], two years after, when in 736 he is recorded to have laid waste the entire country, taken possession of its capital Dunad, burnt a place called Creic, and thrown the two sons of Selbach, Dungal and Feradach, into chains ; and shortly after his son Brude, who had been taken prisoner by Dungal, the king of Dalriada, died. On this occasion Angus appears to have obtained entire possession of Dalriada, and to have driven the two branches of its people, the Cinel Loarn under Muredach and the Cinel Gabhran under Alpin, the brother of Eochaidh, to extremity, for the former appears to have burst from Dalriada upon the Picts who inhabited the plain of Manann between the Carron and the Avon, in a desperate attempt to take possession of their country or to draw Aengus from Dalriada, and was met on the banks of the Avon at Cnuicc Cairpri in Calatros, now Carribber, where the Avon separates Lothian from Calatria, by Talorgan, the brother of Aengus, and defeated and pursued by him with his army, and many of his chief men slain.

The ford at Carribber bears the name of "the fechtin foord," as well as of Redford, which is also the name of a farm adjoining. The word *red* here refers not to the colour of blood, but to the turmoil attending the strife in the "redding" of the quarrel. Redding-muir, where the fighting may be supposed to have commenced, is about three miles off, and Quarrelhead, at Maddiston, fully a mile. Candie, again, which may be the Gaelic *caoineadh*, lamentation, is about a mile from

Redford, and a good mile farther on is Drumbroider, hill of conflict, and farther away is Redbrae. Nearer *linn du,* or the Black Loch, is Redhall; beside the loch is Louis-muir, the muir of encampment, and not far away is Fuehill, the hill of fleeing. There is a large artificial-looking mound near the Neuk, called Castlehill, out of which old weapons have been taken, and there are other mounds in the neighbourhood, probably raised over the dead after this or some other battle.

The lands of Carribber slope down from Bowden to the Avon, and seem to have borne the name thus early. The meaning of Carribber is possibly *Caer-y-bwr,* the fort of the embankment—the slope at the east end of the elsewhere precipitous Bowden being so defended. Bowden, again, may be *Bal-din,* peak-fort, or fort on the hill-top—probably abandoned as such by 736.

The only other historical memorial of the Northumbrian time preserved in the district is an old tradition referred to by Sir Robert Sibbald, that there was in Linlithgow, or its neighbourhood, some stone or erection called " King Cay's Cross,"—supposed to have had some reference to King Achaius (who died 819), the sixty-fifth King of Scotland of the old chroniclers—and which may possibly have been one of those memorials of strife which abounded in the county, it having been for a long time a sort of debatable land.

The name *Lothian* is supposed to be the Saxon word *Lothing,* signifying a border district, and was once applied to the whole coast from the Tweed to the Avon; and Linlithgowshire, Edinburghshire, and Haddingtonshire, are still denominated respectively West, Mid, and East Lothian. The division of West Lothian is very naturally formed by the waters of the Almond on the east, which flows into the Firth of Forth at *Cramond,* a principal port of the Romans, called by them *Alaterva,* and the Avon on the west, which anciently, before the Carse was gained from the sea, joined the Firth at *Inveravon.*

From the time of Malcolm II., who compelled the cession of the Lothians about 1018, through the reigns of Kings Duncan and Macbeth to the accession of Malcolm III. (*Ceanmohr* or bighead) in 1057, there is nothing extant of local interest. It was in Malcolm's reign, in 1066, that William of Normandy invaded England and assumed its crown, and the event has left some record in this neighbourhood in the names of *Port Edgar* and *Queensferry*. The story goes that Edgar Atheling, the heir to the English throne, with his mother and sisters, flying from the invaders, were obliged, by stress of weather, to take refuge with their ships within the quiet waters of the Firth of Forth above Queensferry, and landed at a spot since called Port Edgar. The eldest of the sisters, Margaret, was shortly after married to King Malcolm, and the passage or ferry, from her frequent use of it in her journeys between Dunfermline and the south, came, it is said, to be called by the name of the Queen's ferry. The sheltered waters of the Firth, too, where hundreds of windbound vessels may yet be seen riding in safety, bears the name of *St. Margaret's Hope*, or harbour. The earliest notice of Queensferry is in an Act of Parliament or King's Council of Malcolm IV., 1164, where it is called "portum regine," but the Ferry is called "passagium Inuirkethin" in Acts of the subsequent reign of William the Lion, undated, and of Alexander II., 1227. In the *Legend of St. Andrew*, Hungus, the King of the Picts, is related to have set up the head of the Saxon, Athelstane, on a pole at Ardchinnechun, below "what is now called Portus Reginae," shewing that it had at one time another name. Curiously enough one name of the hilly peninsula on the north side of the firth, now known only as North Queensferry or as the Ferry-hills, has been transferred to the old castle and village of Rossyth, not far off : *Ros* in modern Gaelic meaning peninsula or promontory, *soitheach*, ship, or *sgath*, shelter.

The rivulet, town, and bay of Inverkeithing, on the east and at the back of the *Ros* possibly owe their name to the *cwddyn* or shelter afforded to vessels by the *Ros*, the British name of which might be *Go-ynys-cwddyn*, or partly island, or peninsular shelter, or *Goynys-cyfing*, peninsula of the strait or narrow. Bede, who wrote about the end of the seventh century, says that the Firth of Forth had in the middle of it the city of *Giudi*. It has been assumed from this that Giudi was on an island—in fact on the *Inch* or *ynys* of *Inchkeith*, which forms a natural breakwater about the middle of the Firth. Bede does not say, however, that Giudi was on an island ; and although he says that Alcluith or Dumbarton

C

was on the right hand of the Clyde, he could scarcely describe the peninsula or the town upon it as on the left hand, as it stands right out into the middle of the Firth of Forth. North Queensferry, then, has a fair case for being considered the ancient Giudi. Mr Skene conjectures (*Four Ancient Books of Wales*) that the *Caer Sidi* of Taliessin's poems is the *Giudi* of Bede and *Iudeu* of Nennius. In one of these poems there are eight Caers named, six of them in the refrain of the six divisions — a different one in each of course—"Except seven none returned from the Caer Sidi—Vedwyd—Rigor—Golud—Vandwy—Ochren." These are either different names or descriptions of one and the same Caer, or else names of Caers so connected as to suggest the same expedition. One of the other two is called *Caer Pedryvan.* An old estate near Linlithgow is named Pardovan, and has a "camphill" on it. Roman camps, however, were all or mostly, in the language of the Cymry, *pedryd* or square. Sidi, like Pedryvan, may be descriptive, and be "the chair of the sovereign," described in another poem as standing sheer up out of the water when "the billow covers the shingle." Conjectural etymology is of little value without historical confirmation, but the one sometimes helps out the other. The following may be considered :—

QUEENSFERRY—*Goyngs-for*, Welsh for peninsula passage.

INVERKEITHING—*Inver-cumhann* (pronounced coovann), Gaelic for creek of the strait or narrow.

SOCIETY—*Sgath-tigh* (pronounced skha-tah-o-ye), Gaelic for shelter-house ; *Sidi-ty*, Welsh for Sidi-house.

ARDCHINN-ECHUN—a name not now in use—may be Gaelic *Ard-ceann*, high-head, and Welsh *Eching*, strait or narrow.

The following verse—a literal translation—from Mr Skene's book, is thought to refer to Guidi :—

A pleasant Caer there is on the surface of the ocean.
May be joyful in the splendid festival of its king.
And the time when the sea makes great audacity.
The crowns of bards are usual over mead vessels.
A wave will come, in haste, speed unto it,
That will bring them to the green sward from the region of the Ffieti.
And may I obtain, O God, for my prayer,
When I keep the covenant of conciliation with thee.

The heights, in the few following notes, are taken from the Ordnance Maps, and are given as likely to be of general interest. The high hill to the south of Linlithgow is called *Cocklerue*—sometimes Frenchified into *Cuckold-le-roi*, but the name probably means just, *Ri* being king, the king of cockles or caps or cowls, from its appearance—its summit is 911 feet above the level of the sea; to the west is *Bowden* (749 feet), beyond which lies Torphichen, probably old Celtic *Tor-fugin*, hills for flight, or hills of refuge. The hills to the east of Cocklerue are called *Broomyknowes*, or *Riccarton Hills* (832 feet); and the abrupt crag still farther to the east and south is *Binny Craig* (718 feet). The highest point on this range of eminences and in the county, 1016 feet above the level of the sea, is on Cairnpapple, near Bathgate. The Monument on the hill to the north of the loch commemorates a grand-uncle of the present Earl of Hopetoun, Brigadier-General the Honourable Adrian Hope, who fell in the Indian Mutiny, in 1858, at Rooeah, in Oude. The hill (559 feet) is commonly called *Bonnytoun-hill*, and sometimes *Glower-o'er-em*, from the extensive view it commands, it is supposed. The Welsh *glo-rhwym*, for coal, would almost tempt one to think that there is a reference to the outcrop of the coal measures, which occurs here, and which was worked long ago. No one who has the time to spare should neglect taking a walk round the loch, or to the top of this hill, for both of which walks there are public footpaths. The hill to the north-east, with the tower on its summit, is *Binns* (372 feet), the property of the representatives of General Thomas Dalyell, of Restoration memory, who raised the Scots Greys, and dragooned the Covenanters. A fine portrait of the old General, with his long beard, is preserved at Binns. The tower is an ornamental erection.

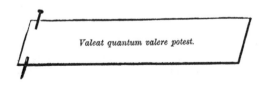

Valeat quantum valere potest.

Remains of Castle of Edward I., and East Front of Palace.

CHAPTER III.

THE CRUSADING TIMES AND WARS OF INDEPENDENCE.

IT is in the reign of David I. (1124–53), fully one hundred years after the Lothians became finally a portion of the Scottish kingdom, that light begins to be thrown, to any considerable extent, on the state and history of the country, by documents, preserved for the most part in the Registers of abbeys and priories. The foundation of both towns and churches, the first mention of which is found in the records of his time, is often erroneously ascribed to David, whose liberal donations of property in his burghs and domains, and of the revenues of churches, to the monasteries, drew from one of his successors the grumbling compliment that he had been "a sair Sanct for the Crown."

His grants here include :—to the abbey of Dunfermline, a

house in the town; to the priory of St. Andrews, the church, with its chapels and lands, as well within burgh as without; and to the abbey of Holyrood, the skins of all the sheep and cattle [made use of] at his Castle, or that should die on his domain, of Linlithgow. In the reign of David, then, we find at Linlithgow, a royal residence; a church dedicated to St. Michael endowed with houses and lands, and with dependent chapels; and a king's burgh, or, as termed in later times, a royal burgh, which had been a seat of population from an unknown antiquity.

It was about 1153, too, that Torphichen became the property and the seat of the principal House in Scotland of the Hospitallers, the famous Knights of St. John of Jerusalem. This and the similar orders, the Templars and the Teutonic Knights, instituted during the first Crusade for the protection and service of pilgrims to the Holy Land, from the great possessions they were endowed with in almost every country in Europe, became powerful bodies, forming, with the troops they were able to maintain, the principal support of the subsequent Crusades. Besides their Preceptory and lands at Torphichen, the Hospitallers held property in the burgh of Linlithgow, and, after the suppression of the Templars in 1312, became possessed of the property originally belonging to that powerful order. Both properties, as well as the manor of Kirkliston, which originally belonged to the Templars, have all been confounded together under the names of Temple-lands and Temple-tenements. Of the Preceptory at Torphichen scarcely a trace remains, though it was a sufficiently extensive erection to accommodate the magnates of the kingdom who adhered to him when assembled under Wallace's Guardianship, as well as to afford accommodation in turn to the retinue of Edward I. An agreement between the Priory of St. Andrews and the Brethren of Torphichen may be found in the Register of St. Andrews (1162–77), whereby the chapel of Torphichen is bound to pay a mark of silver annually to the mother church of Linlithgow as composition for burial dues. The transept, or as popularly styled, "the quier" or choir of a fine church in what is called the early second-pointed style, and some faint traces which are pointed out as foundations of the Preceptory buildings, are all that remain of this once great establishment, except, perhaps, a stone in the churchyard, marking (it has been supposed) the centre of the sanctuary or place of refuge, which extended, it is said, for about a mile round.

From the ecclesiastical records of the twelfth and thirteenth centuries may be gleaned incidentally that there was a school in Linlithgow in 1187, and the fact that a very large portion of the lands in the neighbourhood pertained to the crown. Amongst the private properties we find Ochiltree, which, as we learn from an agreement for erecting a private chapel there, belonged to Alexander, son of William Thoraldson; and Binny was then held by William de Lindsay, the record of whose grant of a piece of land to the church or chapel of St. Giles of Binny, has been preserved. One of the witnesses to this deed bears the name of Turstan, the son of Leving, one of the progenitors, it may be presumed, of the future Earls of Linlithgow and Callendar. The Dundases of Dundas, also, appear, from other sources, to have been settled within the county at even an earlier date.

It was during this period that the burgesses, it is said, were able, in 1290, to found a Carmelite Friary, the third of this order founded in Scotland, and which existed till the Reformation. No vestige of the building now remains, but the place where it stood retains the name of the Friars' Brae, and a modern dwelling-house on their property is still known by the name of the Teind Barn. A new Parish Church was also built in the reign of Alexander II., and dedicated or opened in 1242. It is probable, indeed, as there is no record of any subsequent opening or dedication, that the present structure was then founded, although it has been considerably altered and added to since then. The church was served by a vicar, and the vicar's house stood, as in after times, near the church, on the site, it is believed, of the present Burgh School or of the County Hall. The Rural Deanery of Linlithgow was then, also, nearly co-extensive with the present presbytery of the name. From a short deed by Edward III. of England, while he held this part of the country, granting, in 1335, the custody or keepership of it to a priest of the name of John de Swanlund, we learn that there was a public Hospital then in existence—supposed to have been situated east of the town, where also stood St. Magdalen's Chapel. Emmanuel Convent, for

Bernardine or Cistertian Nuns, was also one of the foundations of this time. It was founded by Malcolm IV., David's
successor, in 1156, and appears to have been then and subsequently within the county or constabulary of Linlithgow. A
small portion of the building yet remains on what is now the
Stirlingshire side of the Avon; and what are now called the
Burgh Mills was one of the gifts of Alexander II. to the Convent. The Convent stood on what is called Manuel Haugh.
About a hundred years ago the Avon came down "in spate,"
and swept away a small village, and the remains of the Convent buildings, all but a solitary ivy-covered gable. A very
perfect example of the church architecture of the first half of
the twelfth century may still be seen in the parish church of
Dalmeny; and one less perfectly preserved, of the fourteenth
century, in the chapel of the Carmelite Friary at South
Queensferry.

The twelfth and thirteenth centuries seem to have been a
period of considerable prosperity in Scotland. The Norman
power and dynasty were not, until near the end of this period,
so firmly rooted in England as to allow its rulers to turn their
attention seriously to the reduction of Wales and Scotland.
Edward I. had but lately completed the conquest of Wales
when Alexander III. was accidentally killed near Kinghorn, in
1286, and his successor, his infant grand-daughter Margaret,
died on the voyage from Norway in 1290, furnishing by the
disputes as to the succession an opportunity for interference
which the able Edward was not slow to take advantage of;
and now ensued that long period of war and devastation
which laid the foundation of the mutual hatred with which
the two countries so long regarded each other; even in 1481
we find the estates of Scotland, in that usually dry and formal
document, an Act of Parliament, describing Edward IV. as
"the Revare Edward calland him king of Ingland." Prior
Winton, who wrote an *Orygynale Chronykil of Scotland*, in
the early part of the fifteenth century, gives a popular rhyme,
often quoted as the earliest specimen of the language in use in
Lowland Scotland in the beginning of the fourteenth century,
and which, at least, gives fit expression to the sad and wistful
feelings with which the people would look back upon the
times byegone :—

> " Quhen Alysander, oure kyng, wes dede,
>   That Scotland led in luwe* and le,†
>   Away we sons‡ of ale and brede,
>   Of wyne in waughts, of gamyn and gle.
>   Our gold was changyd into lede.—
>   Christ, born in-to virgynyte,
>   Succour Scotland, and remede,
>   That stad§ is in perplexyte."‖

Amongst the great families settled in the neighbourhood, we find Sir Nicol de Graham of Abercorn, a relation of Sir John de Graham, also of Abercorn, the friend and companion of Sir William Wallace ; Sir Nicol being the only person from Linlithgowshire who sat in the great Parliament held at Brigham in 1290. In 1296, Sir Nicol re-appears as swearing fealty to Edward I., after the country had, as Edward thought, been finally annexed to England ; William and Freskin de Douglas, and Serle and Saer de Dundas, the progenitors of some of the great families of these names, also appear in the Ragman Roll, as it is called, as well as John Rabuck and John of Mar, the two bailies of the burgh, Andrew the Serjeant, William o the Hulle, John the Porter, Matthew of Kinglas, Henry of the Wro [Wrea], Philip of Abernethy, Gilbert of Hildeclive [Hiltly], William Fitz Ernande [Ernandson], Michael the Lardener, Nicol the Serjeant, the burgesses, and whole community of the burgh.

In two years the exertions of Wallace had cleared the country of Edward's troops, and Wallace is found, in March 1298, issuing his mandates from Torphichen. Edward, returned from Flanders, was soon in Scotland again at the head of a powerful army ; which lay, from the end of June till the 22nd July, stretched along the country, waiting for supplies by sea. On the 22nd of July the battle of Falkirk was fought, in which the Scottish army was routed. Edward is said to have spent

---

* Love.   † Tranquillity.   ‡ Abundance.   § Placed or situated.
‖ Chalmers, in his dissertation on the Scoto-Saxon Language of Scotland, prefixed to his Edition of Sir David Lyndsay's Works, says, " as this song is much more refined than the speech of England at the same period, we must regard it as the language of the chronicler." It is probable, though, that the text is corrupt, as for instance the words of the chronicler are usually quoted, " wine and wax," or sometimes " wine and war," the sense requiring not " wine and *wax*," nor the more absurd " wine and *war*," but, as put above, wine *in waughts*"—in copious draughts, that is, not sparingly.

the night previous to the battle of Falkirk on the Burgh-muir, about a mile east of Linlithgow; and there is a spot in a field to the north of the Blackness road which has been pointed out as the place where his tent was pitched; and the tradition as to the place is not improbable, as it commands an extensive view westward as far as Wallace-stone above Polmont, from which point, as the tradition of the district goes, Wallace viewed the battle, or, which is as likely, contemplated the advance of the English army. On his return from the north, Edward is found again making his head-quarters at Abercorn, on the 15th of August. There is a story, not very explicit as to time, in Blind Harry, to the effect that after the battle of Falkirk, Wallace sent a party headed by "Earl Malcolm" by way of the Carse—

> " To Inneravin the low way to ride,
> That Southren watches might not them espy,
> The other hosts himself led hastily,
> By-the-south Manuel, where they were not seen
> Of the outwatches there had planted been."

And he goes on to relate how the attack was made suddenly, within the town, and ten thousand slain, Edward himself having been nearly taken, and forced to retire to England. This story has met with little credit from our historians. Wallace's name has fixed itself in the neighbourhood of Torphichen, in "Wallace's bed" on the top of Cocklerue, and " Wallace's cave" on the river Avon.

On the occasion of his expedition in 1301, Edward fixed his winter quarters here, and remained over an unusually early winter from 1st November till 31st January following. After this, in the autumn of 1302, he built the castle described by Barbour as "a Pele, mekill and stark"—that is, large and manifestly strong—on the site, it may be presumed, of the old castle; and here, through the mediation of Philip of France, he made a truce with the Scots. In 1303 Edward was back, irresistible as ever, and by 1305, with Wallace slain, Scotland was once more at his feet. A Gascon Knight, Pier or Peter Luband, was, on the settlement of the affairs of the conquered country, left in charge of the castle of Linlithgow, and, it appears from orders of Edward II., had charge under him of the castles of Livingston and Edinburgh also.

Till the hay-harvest of 1313, the castle, and of course the district, remained in possession of the English, though it would appear from the way in which the castle was taken, that the dwellers in the neighbourhood ardently sympathised with the successes of Bruce, who by this time had recovered nearly the whole of Scotland. Through the narratives of historians and story-tellers, the tale of the capture of the castle has become "familiar as a household word." The hero of the story, William Bunnock, was a "husband" or farmer whom the garrison employed because he lived at hand, to lead or drive in the hay from the fields they had in the neighbourhood. He is described by Barbour as "a stout carle and a stour, and of himself dour and hardy," and he appears to have been possessed of some grim humour—telling his employers, on the night before, that in the morning he would bring them "a fothyr"

> "Fayrar and gretar, and weill more
> Than he brocht ony that year before."

Having spoken to some of his neighbours, they agreed that eight of them should lie concealed beneath the hay in the waggon, and that a number more should lie in ambush ready to complete the capture after the gate or entrance had been secured; and, so having arranged, he drove his waggon to the castle, and the porter having opened the gate, Bunnock drove his waggon into the gateway, and crying "Call all! call all!" (the signal agreed on), cut with the hatchet he had provided the soyme or rope fastening the horse, brained the porter, and forthwith the men from the waggon engaged the soldiers left in the castle, and being immediately joined by those who lay in ambush, the place was taken; the remainder of the garrison who were working in the fields, when they learned how matters stood, fleeing, some to Edinburgh and some to Stirling, places which still remained in the possession of the English. Edinburgh Castle was taken shortly after this by Randolph and his daring band, and in one of its dungeons was found Sir Piers Luband, whose fidelity to England had been suspected by the garrison: whether his remissness in allowing the castle here to be taken had anything to do with this it is impossible to say, but he then entered into the Scottish service, and possibly fought at Bannockburn on the right side.

Bunnock of course immediately acquainted King Robert with his success, and was "worthily rewarded" by, it is said, a grant of land in the neighbourhood. The castle Bruce ordered to be demolished—"gert drive it doun to the ground," says Barbour, and no further mention of it has been found until 1350, thirty-seven years after, when David II. is found giving John Cairns, an inhabitant of the town, the liferent of the park round the castle, on condition of his making some necessary repairs on it for the king's coming.

It is highly probable that the demolition of the castle only extended to those extra works reared by Edward during his three months' occupancy. What the nature of these was may be inferred from the style of the other castles which Edward reared to secure his conquests. Here, it would probably be a high and heavy wall, strengthened at intervals by still higher and strongly-built round towers, such as those the remains of which may still be seen at the east side of the palace, and which have been retained as piers for the flying buttresses supporting the wall. The connecting wall, which is five feet thick, has been almost entirely ruined, but portions of the original masonry still remain, easily distinguishable from the patched portions; and the foundation of the wall running westward from the corner tower was laid bare in the course of the recent improvements on the grounds. *Cardonell* recognised these towers as remains of Edward's castle, but almost all subsequent writers have overlooked this. The stone of which the towers have been built has withstood the weather well, a mason's mark being still discernible on the exterior of the large one. The old castle would probably be retained, with any additional buildings necessary, within the new enclosure, and may have been left standing when the fortifications erected by Edward I. were demolished; otherwise, a new castle must have been built by Robert I. or David II. A great crowned head in bold relief was some years ago found in the debris of the older buildings, and is preserved in the small museum of fragments in the Palace. It is in all likelihood the head of Edward I., and it would in all probability surmount the gateway of his castle.

Edward II. is found here, in October 1310, in the course of his expedition of that year; and would pass his ruined castle in June 1314, on his way with his host to relieve Stirling, and back again, his object unaccomplished, with only five hundred horse, and daringly pursued by Douglas with eighty, from the memorable field of Bannockburn.

Once more was the district annexed to England in 1334, during the usurpation of Edward Baliol, in the minority of David II., but though, as has been already mentioned, an order of Edward III. is still in existence having reference to the Hospital of the town, no mention has been found of the castle, from which it may be presumed that it was not re-edified as a "mekill and stark" castle like that of Edward I. That the castle was habitable in the time of David II. has already been noticed.

In the period under review, and for at least three centuries following, the burgh was of some comparative importance amongst the trading communities of the country. "The Chamberlain received that year (1369) of Customs from the burgh of Dunbar, a hundred and fourscore and seventeen pounds. The Customs of Haddington yielded £873; Edinburgh, £3849; Linlithgow, £1403; Stirling, £106; Perth, £710; the City of St. Andrews, £172; Aberdeen, £1100; Dundee, £800; Montrose, £244; Elgin, £71; Inverness, £56; Ayr, £25."* Its situation near Blackness—the safest and most convenient anchorage for shipping in the inner waters of the Firth—was perhaps the principal source of its prosperity, the burgh having the exclusive right of exporting or importing goods on the shore of the Firth from Cramond to the Avon. It was on account of its being the most advanced position in convenient proximity to the sea, as much as from other considerations, that Edward I. fixed upon it as a place for his head-quarters in this district. Linlithgow appears, by Thomas Lethe, in the first Scotch Act of Parliament in which the representatives of burghs are enumerated, in 1366, along with the burghs of Edinburgh, Aberdeen, Perth, Dundee, Montrose, and Haddington; and, as has been already mentioned, Lanark and Linlithgow were taken, in 1368, into the Court of the Four Burghs in place of Berwick and Roxburgh, then in possession of the English.

---

* Innes' *Scotland in the Middle Ages.*

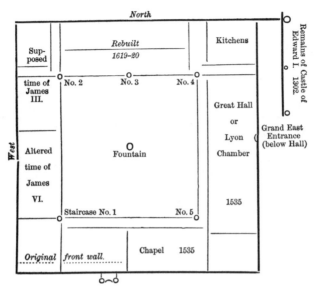

General Plan of Principal Floor of Palace.

CHAPTER IV.

THE STEWARTS AND THE DOUGLASES.

THE line of the great Bruce was now to be succeeded by that of the brilliant but unfortunate Stuarts. The Douglases—the descendants of the "good Sir James" who had fought so well under King Robert—were now growing into a great and powerful house, with aspirations after supreme power in the state; and these aspirations, the extinction of the direct line of the Bruce, seemed a fit opportunity for realising. At this period and afterwards, down to the forfeiture of the "Black Douglases" in the reign of James II., they held extensive estates in this neighbourhood; and it was here that Earl William convoked his vassals and adherents, and proclaimed his intention of disputing the title of the

Steward. The combination, however, of the Stewards' supporters, who immediately advanced under Sir Robert Erskine, obliged the Earl to abandon the attempt; and the subsequent marriage of the Earl's eldest son to King Robert's daughter, Isabella, and other concessions, had to satisfy, for the time, the ambition of the Douglases.

The Stewards were before this connected with the district, having lands at Bathgate, and a castle, the site of which is still pointed out near that town; and with Robert II. the castle of Linlithgow appears to have been a frequent residence. He is found in 1384 contributing 26s. 8d. to the building or repairing of the church tower, and in August 1388 holding a Council-General or Parliament here. The earliest charter in the possession of the burgh, granting to the community the mails, firms, or rents hitherto drawn by the King's chamberlain, for an annual payment of five pounds sterling,* was given while he was residing in the castle in October 1389. The castle appears, also, to have been one of the principal residences of Robert III., who is found holding a Parliament here in 1399. The only other events of which history has preserved any record in connection with the place for the next thirty years, are the facts that the town was destroyed by fire in 1411, and again in 1424, the year in which James I. returned from his long captivity in England. In the fire of 1424, the Church and the Castle, or Palace as it is termed in the account of this catastrophe, also suffered. Mr Dickson, in his preface to Vol. I. of the *Accounts of the Lord High Treasurer of Scotland*, informs us that preparations for rebuilding the palace were made in 1425, and that on to 1430 the sum of £2440, 10s. 7½d. was expended, under the direction of John of Walton, as Master of Work; and that "under the superintendence of his

---

* The following extract from a letter of Mr Robertson's, clears up this subject—one which popular writers on antiquities do not seem to have properly understood hitherto :—"Chalmers's distinction between a royal burgh and a king's town in demesne is a distinction which had no existence in Scotland in that age. It may or may not have had a charter; but a charter was not necessary to its existence as a burgh, although convenient as evidence of the fact. It was not until King Robert Bruce's reign, that the crown began to lease out burghs to the corporation or community of the burgh, at fixed rents. Before that time every burgess paid his own individual rent for the burgh land which he held, to the King's Chamberlain, who for that purpose visited the burgh every year."

successors, Robert Wedale, Robert Livingstone, John Holmes, and John Weir, work continued to be done," through the reign of James I. who was murdered in 1437, and in the reign of James II. till 1451.

The power and pride of the Douglases reached their highest point in the reign of James II., when it came to be virtually a question of who should be king. In this neighbourhood, they held the castles of Inveravon, Blackness, and Abercorn. Blackness was burnt or destroyed in 1443, by Crichton the Chancellor, in the raid he made on their lands here, during the minority of the king. Inveravon was reduced by James himself, in 1454, and left in ruins;* and Abercorn, the strongest of the three, and, according to Buchanan, the strongest of the whole of their castles, was reduced, after an arduous siege of a month's duration, in the beginning of 1455. This last and crowning victory of a somewhile dubious war, was commemorated, as Buchanan put it, by leaving the castle half-demolished for its monument.

Of the castle of Abercorn, only a circular mound remains, marking the position possibly of one of its round towers, the fragments of its walls having been removed or covered up when the grounds around Hopetoun House were laid out. It stood on a sort of peninsula, crowning the steep sea-bank. Of Inveravon castle, which, from a similar position, overlooked the Carse of Falkirk, and commanded the lowest ford on the Avon, only the fragment of a round flanking tower remains; and all tradition of its having been, four hundred years ago, a castle of the Douglases, having been lost, it remained, until Tytler published the facts as recorded in the *Auchinleck Chronicle*, a puzzle to antiquaries: the most popular account being, that it was a Roman watch-tower on the line of the great wall. Blackness castle was by-and-bye rebuilt, and it has recently been converted into a gunpowder magazine and military store.

Blackness castle appears to have remained in ruins for some time after the downfall of the Douglases, it having been

---

* There are indications of Roman fortification immediately below the ruin; and the road leading downward cuts through an ancient shell heap or "kitchen midden" of great size, heaped against the old sea bank, and also cuts through a Roman causeway.

granted by a charter under the great seal in 1465, to the burgh of Linlithgow, for the constructing of a new port or pier at Blackness, with power to make use, for this purpose, of the stones of the castle, which was to be razed to the ground, and the hill and rock, from St Ninian's Chapel to the sea, all round the promontory, were to belong in future to the burgh. The principal reason given for this grant was the "vexations, troubles, harassments, and extortions" formerly practised by those who held the castle, upon the merchants of the burgh and others frequenting the port. The building of a new pier may have been carried into effect, but the grant itself seems to have been recalled by the act of 1476, revoking all grants made in the minority of James III., and especially of such places as were considered to be "keys of the kingdom." On the top of the castle-hill of Blackness are still traceable the foundations of a building, about 150 feet in length, by from 30 to 40 in width, regarding which no tradition can be found, and which may possibly have been part of the early castle—the succeeding one having been built on the projecting rocks, almost entirely within high-water mark. In 1481 an English fleet burnt the shipping at Blackness, and, one account says, the castle also. If it was destroyed it must have been quickly rebuilt, as it is found in use as a state-prison in 1489.

The lands of the Douglases in this neighbourhood were now conferred upon the Hamiltons, whose desertion from the Douglases at a critical time had been of material benefit to the King's cause; and considerable portions of them still remain in the possession of their descendants.

It would appear that the burgesses of Linlithgow had been faithful supporters of the crown through all these troubles, as well as sufferers by them; the charter of 1451, freeing them from payment of duties on salt and skins, being evidently intended as a compensation for their losses.

The minority of James III., who was left under the care of his mother and the good Bishop Kennedy, was passed to a considerable extent peacefully at Linlithgow, one of the domains and palaces usually assigned for the residence and support of the Queens-Dowager. Henry VI. of England, when dislodged from the throne of Edward IV., seems to have been indebted to the Queen for a temporary residence here in 1460.

The forcible seizure of the King's person, and the power it conferred, which ended so fatally for the Livingstons in the former reign, was now about to be repeated by the Boyds, and with like results; and it was after the Queen and the wise old Kennedy were dead, and Lord Livingston held rule as chamberlain, that the faction headed by the Boyds formed the resolution, which they carried into effect while the king sat in his Exchequer Court in the Palace, of carrying him off and assuming the government of the country.

An old historian says of James III. that "he was much given to buildings, and repairing of chappels, halls, and gardens, as usually are the lovers of ease; and the rarest frames of churches and palaces in *Scotland* were mostly about this time." James was married to Margaret of Denmark, who brought Orkney and Shetland for her tocher, in 1467. In the same year building operations were recommenced on the Palace, "and during the next four years considerable sums were again expended upon it. In 1468 the grounds surrounding the palace were extended by the purchase of thirty-five perches of ground east of the King's house, from several persons, for the sum of £19, 17s. 8d." Information such as this from the Exchequer Rolls and the Treasurer's Accounts has till now been practically unattainable, consequently architects who have written books on the palace have written very much in the dark, and have wisely confined themselves mostly to the work of the time of James V. and VI. Any remarks on this subject here hazarded are of course to some extent conjectural.

In the palace, the lower parts at least of the north-west corner, and the northern part of the west side, have been credited to James III. One of the rooms, indeed, has been long shown as his bedroom, and although this is not much to count on it is not unlikely. The apartment has been much altered, as may be seen from an inspection of the fine groining of the ruined window, and of what has been converted into a closet, close beside it. The bosses of the groining are carved with the device of an unicorn reposing under a tree, two of them encircled with the motto BELLE A VOUS·LEULE—probably old French for *fair be your rising* or *waking*. Curiously enough the same motto was recently found scratched in black letter on the plaster of the side of a window in the south front wall of the palace. The window had been built up when the additional thickness was added to the front to bring this part of the palace in line with the chapel. The groining in the apartment below the bedroom is worthy of attention. The oldest-looking masonry of the palace (always excepting the old round towers at the north-east) is apparently on the west side. On this side there are indications that the old style of architecture common in town dwellings, of wooden galleries in front of the more solid stone building, was at one time in use. A careful examination of the walls will show where the wooden beams entered; and the supposition that this style of architecture was used, and abandoned, accounts for the bareness of the west side of the palace. No picture or record of the old style of the north side having been preserved, it is useless to hazard a conjecture as to the builder. The entrance porch of the south side and the original walls within both the present exterior and interior walls may be fairly credited to James I. and James II.

The process of church and cathedral building was generally a slow one, or rather while funds came in, a never-ceasing one —where no increase of size was required, the old was rebuilt in newer style. We have seen King Robert in 1384 contributing his mite towards the building of the steeple, and it is not improbable that it was not finished till the time of James III., or a new one even may have been erected. The architectural style of the church—the Scottish Decorated, as it is called—is that which prevailed during this time. There can be little doubt about the finishing at least of the steeple, as the open crown on the top had for a finial the uncommon one of a hen for a vane, with chickens dispersed on the points below—an adaptation of a favourite device of James III. The device was a hen with her chickens under her wings, and the motto NON DORMIT QUI CUSTODIT—*he sleeps not who guards.*[*]

The pacification of Blackness is the next prominent historical incident which occurs in the neighbourhood during the reign

---

[*] *Historic Devices*, by Mrs Bury Palliser, author of this and of many other interesting works.

of James III.; and this was followed shortly afterwards by the assembling of Angus, old " Bell-the-cat," the chief of the " Red Douglases," with the Humes, the Hepburns, and their adherents, with " the prince " nominally at their head; and here they " made proclamation to all manner of men that would come and defend the prince." The battle of Saughie and the slaughter of the King followed; and the conspirators returned here next day, still uncertain whether the prince were now James IV. In the distribution of offices under the new government are found the Vicar of Linlithgow, one of the Hepburns, clerk of the rolls and council, and Sir William Knollys, lord St. John, treasurer to the King.

The church steeple, recently finished, was now to be furnished with a finer and larger bell than the two older ones it possessed. A remarkably fine-toned one of about half-a-ton weight was got—from the low countries it may be presumed. It bears, in addition to the royal arms, a copy of the old seal of the burgh, and the inscription—X **Lynlithqw . billa . me . fecit . bocor . alma . maria . domini . jacobi . quarti . tempore . magnifici . Anno . milleno . quadringeno . nonageno.*** On the lower margin is the monogram, which forms the tail-piece to this chapter.†

The Treasurer's Accounts contain much interesting information. Mr Dickson in his preface says, " the portion of the palace erected between 1488 and 1496 appears to have been in the south side, as the mention of timber for the roof of the chapel indicates that it formed part of the new building [or alteration or rebuilding, for there have been three successive roofs on the chapel]. In 1491 there was expended on the building of the palace £503, 19s. 3d., and on the park dyke £145, 0s. 8d., and in the next six months, £129, 3s., besides £100 for timber." The two north-corner staircases, on the

---

* " The Town of Linlithgow made me, in the reign of the august Lord, James the Fourth, in the year one thousand four hundred and ninety. I am called Blessed Mary." The second bell, re-cast in 1773, bears only the names of the founders, and a copy of both sides of the town's large seal. The third, re-cast in 1718, is called " SICUT QUONDAM [as formerly] MEG DUNCAN."

† If this monogram be not the founder's, it (according to the Rev. J. T. Fowler, of Durham, who has given special attention to this department of Antiquarian research) may be " 1. That it is the name of Christ, although this was usually χρc or χρς, and I have never seen χi on anything ancient. 2. That it is an indication of the weight, ten— ? or of the musical note? in some German method that I do not understand."

wester one of which is what is called "Queen Margaret's
Bower," are not improbably part of the work done at this
time.   There are many entries of money given to the masons
for drink-silver, whenever the King came; and when here, of
his donations to the altars in the church; to the church
building funds; for the late King's "dyrige and sawle mass;"
and to the Friars; and his benefactions to the poor are frequent and liberal.   The town's folk seem to have practised on
his freehandedness by getting him to stand sponsor for their
children, at least he does so on two occasions.

Item, on Sonda the xxx[ti] da Octobris [1491], in Lythgow, til Hew Hamiltonis
    barne, at [that] the King hwfe [heaved or held up],   .   .   .   lx li.
Item, to put in the candil .   .   .   .   xiiij s.

These great houses, only occasionally used, were not com-
pletely furnished, and payments for carrying back and forward the cupboards, or chests with the silver plate, chapel
furnishings and other things, and by and bye of the King's
Organ or "pair of organs" as it was called, which was carried
back and forward from Edinburgh by two men, are regular
entries.   The glass of the windows seems to have been per-
manent by this time, but there are payments for bringing the
"Arress claythes" or tapestry from Edinburgh, and for hooks
and rings for hanging it up.   The larger floors were thus provided for :—

Item, to Lylle for resschis to the Haw off Lythqow the tyme of the Imbassa-
    touris   .   .   .   .   v s.

James IV. seems to have been partial to spending Pasche
(Easter) and Yule at Linlithgow.   These were times of holi-
day.   These were the days for "Patrik Johnson and the
playaris of Lythgow that playt to the King," and for Blind
Harry the Minstrel, and for "Wallass that tells the geistis
[exploits, tales, or romances] to the King," and for the fithelars,
and harpers, and trumpatouris, and lutaris; for the "gysaris
that dansyt to the King," and even for the priests and others,
who sing "a ballat to the King in the morning;" and for any
tambronaris and spelaris (rope dancers) that came the way.
The following items may be locally interesting :—

Item, to the skynnar of Lythgow for halkgluvis to the King,   .   .   xviij s.
Item, to Willyeam Sangstare of Lythqow for a sang bwke he brocht to the
    King, be a precep, ...   x li.

Item, the xiij day of November, to Brownhyll cordynar, for the Kingis werk, ... vi li.

Item, till a man that gydit the King owre the Mure of Sclamanane, . vi d.

Item, till a wife at Baythcat bog, at the King revit a rong fra, . . xviii d.

Item, the xxjo August, in Lythgow, to Downy, falconar and his man to pass to lwre thare halkis, x dais waigis, ... xviij s.

Item, the last day of September, in the Blackness, quhen the King hard mass there, to the priest, ... ix s.

Item, til a soutar that sewyt halk hwdis to the King, . . . ij s.

Item, on Frida the first day of October, in Torfyching, to the King to play, viij angellis, ... ix li. xij s.

Amongst the memoranda preserved in the Treasurer's Accounts are sundry donations to the Chapel of St. Ninian here, one of which is, "1507, Nov. 26, Item, to the priest of Sanct Ninianes chapell to theke it, xiii sh." This was a chapel, whether built at this time or previously existing is not known, which was situated at the West-port of the town; and which must, not very long after, have gone to decay, as it is described in the charter disposing of it, in 1562, as having been for many years in ruins. St. Ninian was a favourite saint of King James IV., and there are frequent entries in the Treasurer's books of gifts to the priests of St. Ninian's Chapel here, at Blackness, and at Stirling. Some stones with what is called the chapel mark and the plain circular arch of a doorway of the Blackness chapel are preserved, near the original position, in the walls of a barn at Blackness.

It would appear that the population of the town had increased at this time, as very probably had that of the country generally. There is a document of date 1492, in the Burgh Charter-chest, wherein the King grants to the community a rood of land from the Peel to increase the size of the church-yard, and binds them at the same time to build a stone-wall to stop the passage to the Peel and gardens.

The only other memorable events recorded of the reign of James IV. in connection with Linlithgow, are the birth of James V. in the Palace, 10th April 1512; and one of the now seemingly ludicrous attempts to awe the King into the abandonment of the expedition which ended so disastrously at Flodden in 1513.* The following is the quaint account of this

* Among those who fell at Flodden was a Cornwall, laird of Bonhard, here, who it is said was one of six dressed up in the same style as the King, to whom he bore a great resemblance. The family is now extinct, and their town

transaction by Lindsay of Pitscottie.   Scott's metrical version will be found in the Appendix.

The King came to *Lithgow*, where he happened to be for the time at the Council, very sad and dolorous, making his Devotion to God to send him good Chance and Fortune in his Voyage.   In this mean Time, there came a Man clad in a blue Gown in at the Kirk-Door, and belted about him in a Roll of Linen-Cloth : a pair of Brotikins on his Feet, to the Great of his Legs, with all other Hose and Clothes conform thereto ; but he had nothing on his Head, but syde [long] red yellow Hair behind, and on his Haffits [cheek-blades], which wan down to his Shoulders ; but his Forehead was bald and bare.   He seemed to be a Man of two and fifty Years, with a great Pyke-Staff in his Hand, and came first forward among the Lords, crying and speiring for the King, saying, *He desired to speak with him.*   While at the last, he came where the King was sitting in the Desk at his Prayers : But when he saw the King, he made him little Reverence or Salutation, but leaned down groflins [gruffly] on the Desk before him, and said to him in this Manner, as after follows.   *Sir King, my Mother hath sent me to you, desiring you not to pass, at this Time, where thou art purposed ; for, if thou does, thou wilt not fare well in thy Journey, nor none that passeth with thee.   Further she bade thee mell with no Woman, nor use their Counsel, nor let them touch thy Body, nor thou theirs ; for if thou do it, thou wilt be confounded and brought to Shame.*

By this Man had spoken thir Words unto the King's Grace, the Even-Song was near done ; and the King paused on thir Words, studying to give him an Answer : But, in the mean Time, before the King's Eyes, and in the presence of all the Lords that were about him for the Time, this Man vanished away, and could noways be seen nor comprehended, but vanished away as he had been a Blink of the Sun, or a Whip of the Whirlwind, and could no more be seen.   I heard say, *Sir David Lindesay* Lyon Herauld, and *John Inglis* the Marshal, who were, at that Time, young Men, and special Servants to the King's Grace, were standing presently beside the King, who thought to have laid Hands on this Man, that they might have speired further Tidings at him : But all for nought ; they could not touch him ; for he vanished away betwixt them, and was no more seen.

James V. was little more than a year old when his father fell at Flodden, and the usual unsatisfactory state of affairs ensued, from the rival pretensions of the nobility to the possession of power.   A small siege of the palace (about 1517), when Sir Anthony D'Arcy De-la-Bastie was one of the eight Regents, during the absence of Albany, is narrated by Pits-

---

house has been very recently rebuilt.   It was a narrow house of the time of the Charleses, retaining some fragments of an older erection.   Elaborate stucco work on the ceilings was common at this time, and the centre ornament of one of the rooms was the head of Alexander, the hero of the family, who fell at Flodden.   He wears a plumed helmet, and displays an open palm on his left breast.   Some cellars of the older date are still retained, and a stone with date 1527, and the motto " VE' BIG YE SEE VARLY " [we build you see warily].   A metal plate, affixed to the stone, bore the device of a bird with a stalk of *corn* in its mouth, standing on the top of a *wall*.

cottie. The occasion was the murderous attack of Luke
Stirling upon Meldrum of Binns (Binns in Fife)—the "Squire
Meldrum" of Sir David Lindsay—near Holyrood, when De-la-
Bastie followed Stirling's party here and compelled them to
surrender.

The Douglases, under the popular cognomen of "the Red
Douglases," from the fair complexion of the Angus branch of
this great house, rose once more into power in 1525, with
possession of the King, who was now about thirteen. The
first attempt to displace them was made by the Earl of Arran,
who advanced to Linlithgow, in the neighbourhood of which
the various families of the Hamiltons had large estates.
They mustered a force of about five thousand men, but were
immediately obliged to disperse, by the prompt advance of
Douglas with the King at the head of a superior force. The
bold stroke of declaring, by Act of Parliament, the King no
longer a minor, leaving the former Act as to the keeping of
the King's person in force, shortly followed; and now Angus
and the Douglases were the masters or the tyrants of the
state, with all its patronage distributed amongst themselves
and their adherents, and no man daring to say that a Douglas's
man did wrong.

The King, taken from the schools, and from his well-loved
familiar servitor Sir David Lindsay, endured the thraldom
of the Douglases with great impatience. The unsuccessful
attempt of Scott of Buccleugh to effect his deliverance was
followed shortly after by a more formidable one by the
Queen's party, headed by the Earl of Lennox. Assembling a
force of ten thousand men at Stirling, they marched towards
Edinburgh to try conclusions with the Douglases, and were met
about a mile west from Linlithgow by the Earl of Arran with
a body of the Hamiltons, who were now in league with Angus.
Arran held the bridge over the Avon, below which for some
distance the passage of the river was not easily practicable,
with the steep banks which bend round Manuel Haugh, above;
and Lennox was under the double disadvantage of fording the
river and forcing the heights between Manuel Convent and
the bridge. Angus, to whom word had been sent of the
meeting, came quickly to the assistance of Arran. Sir George
Douglas followed with the King, whose sympathy with Len-

nox was so little concealed, that his conductor was tempted to tell him that "Before the enemy shall take thee from us, if thy body should be torn in pieces, we shall have a part." Angus fought with the division under the Earl of Glencairn, and the Hamiltons with that under Lennox, and both Lennox and Glencairn were defeated. Glencairn's life was saved by Andrew Wood of Largo, who was despatched by the King to stop the slaughter, but Lennox, after having surrendered to the Laird of Pardovan, was slain by Sir James Hamilton of Finnart. The spot where Lennox fell was afterwards marked by a heap of stones long known as Lennox's Cairn. One of the hillocks is still known as the Peace-knowe or Peace-hill—a corruption of the Gaelic *Bas*, death. The name is possibly older than this battle. The viaduct of the Edinburgh and Glasgow Railway crosses the battlefield, and many bones and stone-slab coffins, with swords and other weapons, were disinterred while the works were in progress. One of the swords found has been lodged in the small museum of burgh antiquities. It has a pointed blade about $20\frac{1}{2}$ inches long, ornamented with a little engraved scrolling on one side, and the motto PONO LEGES VIRTUTE—*I maintain the laws by valour*. After the battle, the King, with "the Earl of Angus, the Lord Hamilton, with the Humes and Kers, went all that night to Linlithgow, and remained there in great merriness: but the King was very sad and dolorous."

This battle was fought in September 1526, and it was not till May 1528 that the King so cleverly escaped from Falkland. The sadness and dolour were on the side of the Douglases at Linlithgow on the night they turned bridle at Stirling after their fruitless pursuit of their lost prize.

Monogram on large Bell of Church.

Cross Well.

CHAPTER V.

JAMES V., HALY KIRK, AND THE REFORMATION.

JAMES V., now his own master, and in many respects
worthy of being so, commenced a vigorous course of
administration which soon restored order and security
to the country. His own experience of the rule of his nobility
prompted him to shield the people from oppression, and to
raise them politically; and this, combined with his free and

joyous nature, made him a popular favourite—" The King of
the Commons."   His actual reign, from 1528, when he escaped
in his seventeenth year from Falkland, till his death at the
same place in 1542, a period of fourteen years, is one of the
most important and interesting periods in the history both of
Europe and of Scotland.   It is to be regretted, however, that
in the stormy times which followed, the local records of the
transactions of the period have been mostly destroyed; though
some valuable fragments have been preserved.

Amongst these are some of the Minutes of the Burgh-courts,
Treasurer's Accounts, and copies of various documents.   The
Court Book extends from 1529 pretty consecutively till 1534;
there are a few dates in 1536, 7, 8, and 9; then from October 1,
1540, till May 23, 1543, it is nearly entire.   These fragments
have been gathered together and bound up in one volume,
along with a very few leaves of 1563-64, and subsequent
dates.   There occurs on a page containing a sett of the
Common Lands, of date 1564, the following note, subscribed
by the whole Council :—

Die penultima Maii, 1564.   The whilk day this buke being producit in
Counsal, it wes fundin that the marrow of it is revin out, as appears.   And
this we testify be our hand writts.

The history of the country explains sufficiently how this would
be; but it is doubtful whether the destruction would proceed
from rival parties wishing to obliterate the remembrance of
defeat, or from canny burgesses anxious to screen themselves
from the consequences, by destroying the evidence of their
own acts.   Whichever way it was, they have managed to
preserve most of what related to the material interests of the
community.

From these records it would appear that the King was an
annual resident in the Palace in the early part of his actual
reign, the Lyon Herald, or Lion-king-of-arms, who would,
from the nature of his office, be a constant attender at Court
wherever it might be for the time, appearing frequently as a
member of the Town Council.   As these notices throw some
light both on the movements of the King, and upon the history
of Sir David Lindsay, on whom the office of "Harauld to our
sovourain Lord," as he styles himself, was about this time
conferred, the dates of the various entries in which the Lyon

Herald appears sitting are subjoined.* Edinburgh, Stirling,
Linlithgow, and Falkland, appear to have been the principal
royal residences at this time, as enumerated in Sir David's

FAREWELL OF THE PAPINGO.

Adew Edinburgh, thou heich triumphand toun
Within whose boundis richt blythful have I bene,
Of trew merchandis, the rute of this regioun,
Most reddy to ressave court, king and queen ;
Thy policie, and justice may be sene,
Wer devotioun, wysedome, and honestie,
And credence, tint [lost], they may be found in the.

Adew fair Snawdoun [Stirling], with thy towris hie,
Thy chapill royall, park, and tabill round,
May, June, and July, wald I dwell in the,
War I ane man, to heir the bird-is sound ;
Quhilk doith agane thy royall rocke resound.
Adew Lithgow, whose palyce of plesance,
Micht be ane pattern, in Portugall or France.

Fare weill, Falkland, the forteress of Fyfe,
Thy polite park, under the Lowmond Law :
Some time in the, I led ane lustie lyfe,
The fallow deir, to se them raik [run] on raw.
Court-men to cum to the, they stand greit aw,
Sayand, thy burgh bene, of all burrow-is baill, [worst]
Because, in the, they never gat gude aill.

The great improvements in the Palace referred to in Chapter
I. appear to have been made in anticipation of the King's
marriage with the Princess Magdalene of France. These improvements consisted in the remodelling of the east and south
sides of the Palace. On the east side, the great Hall, called
in the records the Lyon Chamber, a spacious apartment of 98½
feet in length by 30 in breadth, with side walls 35 feet in
height, was raised on the foundations of an older structure.
Whether the entrance on this side was then opened or whether
it existed before this is not known. On the south side the
walls of the Chapel were raised, and the five long narrow
windows formed. The passage galleries, the square-headed

---

* 1529, Oct. 4, 15, Nov. 5 ; 1530, Aug. 25, Oct. 3 ; 1531, Oct. 2 ; 1532, June
18, Sept. 15 ; 1533, Oct. 6 ; 1534, Oct. 5 ; 1535, Oct. 5, 9 ; 1536, Oct, 2, 6 ;
few dates preserved till 1540, in which year he does not appear ; 1541, Oct. 7 ;
1542, Oct. 2, 11. There is very little preserved after May 23, 1543, till March
17, 1620, at which date the present series of Council Minute-Books commences.
The general elections took place in October.

mullioned windows of which form so prominent a feature of
the inner court, it is said, were also laid-to, the older wall
being still distinguishable inside of part of them, as well as
inside of the entrance porch. The fine gateway at the head
of the Kirkgate is also believed to be an erection of this date.
It was ornamented over the archway with four carved panels,
representing the collars and jewels of the orders of St. Michael,
the Golden Fleece, and the Garter, orders of knighthood which
were conferred upon King James by Francis, King of France;
Charles V., Emperor of Germany; and Henry VIII., King of
England. The fourth panel, it is said, was filled in with the
collar and jewel of the order of the Thistle, the foundation of
which order has been ascribed to James V.* The elaborate
and finely sculptured fountain in the Palace court is also
believed to be an erection of this date; and the Cross-well of
the town was in all probability erected at this time.† The
principal figure represents St. Michael, and the other figures
are supposed to be representative of his angels, as embodied
in the clergy of Haly Kirk. The people were making fun of
their religion, and the Reformation was well nigh ripe.

The Palace was now "translated" as Pitscottie phrases it,‡
and resplendent with painting and gold; and Lithgow as one
of "the worthy and principal towns" was preparing also for
the proper reception of the Queen. Poor Magdalen's death
delayed this event, but when James in 1539 brought Mary of

---

* These panels were about thirty years since very beautifully restored.
They are not copies, but are very likely not far from the original designs. A
shield with the arms of each of the princes is inserted within the collar. As
the mottoes of the various orders are carved in a style unreadable by the
majority of visitors, the mottoes, so far as the writer can ascertain them, are
subjoined :—The motto of the Thistle, NEMO ME IMPUNE LACESSIT—*No one
may meddle me with impunity;* of the Garter, HONI SOIT QUI MAL Y PENSE—
Evil be to him who evil thinks; of the Golden Fleece, PRÆTIUM NON VILE—*No
ignoble Reward;* of the Cockle, or, as commonly named, from the jewel
attached, of St. Michael, TREMOR IMMENSI OCEANI—*The troubling of the great
deep.*

† It appears from a minute of council of 1628, that the Cross-well was then
standing out of repair " as ane deid monument." It was repaired at that
time, water being procured from the source by which it is still supplied, it
having apparently been supplied originally from the same source as the
fountain in the Palace.

‡ It is from a misapprehension of this phrase, it may be presumed, that
Pinkerton asserts that James V. changed the site of the Palace.

Guise to her future dwelling, the Queen rewarded him for all his cost and labours by declaring that she "had never seen a more princely Palace." The "players of Lythgow" were in request once more, and Sir David Lyndsay's "Satyre of the Three Estaitis," was one of the dainty dishes set before the Queen in January 1540. Of all the royal houses, that of Linlithgow, "the King's great Palace," as it is termed in a subsequent act of parliament, was the most esteemed as a residence by Mary of Guise. Within its walls she gave birth on the 7th of December 1542, to her ill-fated daughter Mary, who, by the death of her father, became Queen of Scots on the 13th of the same month.

In the year that James V. was born (1512) Martin Luther acquired his degree of D.D., and he published his ninety-five theses in opposition to Tetzel in 1517. In the year after James's emancipation (1529) the princes of Germany who supported Luther gave in their famous protest against the edict of Worms which had placed him under the ban of the empire. A new element in politics had been developed, more powerful than any heretofore known to James's predecessors, and he and his race were doomed to extinction in their futile attempts to suppress it. The Reformation had begun. It was here, probably, that Patrick Hamilton, the first martyr of the Scottish Reformation, received the elements of his education. His father, Sir Patrick Hamilton (an illegitimate son of the Lord Hamilton who helped to turn the scale in the contest between James II. and the Douglases) was appointed by James IV., Sheriff of Linlithgow and Captain of the Castle of Blackness in 1498, and at the same time obtained a grant of the King's lands of Kincavel, about a mile and a half east from the town of Linlithgow. He owned, besides, the lands of Stanehouse, in Lanarkshire, and Patrick was, according to Professor Lorimer, born most probably at Glasgow.* However this may be, the offices which his father held would necessitate his frequent residence at Kincavel, and if so, his sons would most probably be educated at the Burgh School. The Court Book opens only in 1529, but in one of the minutes of

---

* See appendix to Professor Lorimer's *Life of Patrick Hamilton*, which contains some extracts from the Burgh Records above referred to ; as well as the copy of the Chaplain's Bond which follows in the text.

that year "William Hamiltoune in Kyncavil; Alex. Hamiltoune in the Grange; and George Hamiltoune in the Medop," are found sitting, as if such matter had special interest for them, on the assize, and amongst other business taking Mr Fynlaw Forest (the Rector it may be presumed) to task, for not keeping a "sufficiande grammariar" to assist him in the school. Patrick after studying at the "Scholis of Art and Jure," in Paris, where the writings of the reformers were well known, returned to Scotland and had to flee to Germany in 1527, where he made the acquaintance and profited by the instructions of Luther, Melancthon, and the other reformed Doctors. Returning in 1528, and while residing at Kincavel, he is said to have been a zealous preacher in the neighbourhood. The King was yet in the keeping of the Douglases, and Archbishop Beaton kept watch in St Andrews over the interests of the Church, which were endangered by widely spread importations of Bibles and other heretical books; and now that to the books were to be added preachers, and these men of rank and influence, a decided step was necessary to arrest the progress of heresy : and so Patrick Hamilton was sent for to a conference at St Andrews, and was there tried, condemned, and burnt, on the last day of February 1528. Sir James Hamilton, Patrick's eldest brother, who now filled his father's offices—(the father perished in the affray in the High Street of Edinburgh called "cleanse the causeway" in 1520)—had assembled a force to rescue his brother, but was prevented by stress of weather from crossing the Firth of Forth until it was too late; so the Sheriff and his men had to return, and by-and-bye had to destroy, it may be, even their own record of the expedition.

The next martyr of the Scottish Reformation on record was Henry Forrest, a young Benedictine monk of St Andrews, and a native of Linlithgow. One family of Forrests about this time seem to have been proprietors of Pardovan, which adjoins Kincavel; and this Henry may have been a son of that Laird of Pardovan to whom Lennox surrendered at Linlithgowbridge. However this may be, it is not unlikely that, being about the same age and belonging to the same place as Hamilton, an intimacy and sympathy would exist between them. He is said to have made some indignant remarks on

Hamilton's execution, and he shared the same fate, the crime of which he was accused being that he possessed a New Testament in English.

From 1528 to 1534 the King appeared to lean towards the side of the Reformation. The dissoluteness of the higher clergy was fitly matched by the ignorance and worthlessness of the priests and monks, and a change of some kind was inevitable. There is very distinct evidence of an attempt, in which Sir James Hamilton of Finnart, and Sir James Hamilton of Kincavel, are found taking part, at a sort of reformation in church matters here, by the Town Council, as may be seen in the extracts from the minutes given in the appendix to Professor Lorimer's work. The sort of morality expected from the ordinary priests is very well shown in the terms of a Chaplain's Bond, the original of which has been preserved in the Burgh Charter-chest.

Til al and sundrie quhais knawledge thir present lettres sal to cum, Patric Brone, chapellane, greting in the Salviour of all. Yhour universite [you all] sal knaw me to be oblist and be thir present lettres, in the faith of my body, leleli and treuli obliss me til honorable and worschipful men, the baileyheis and communitie of the burgh of Linlithgw for thare suppli and favoure done to me thankfulli, that I sal be lele and trew to tham, obedient and inclinand to thare ordinance in all lefful things and honest, tuiching the service of God and haly kirk. In manere as eftir followis. In the first, I obliss me to do divine service at the altar of Corpus Christi, foundat in the parisch kirk of Llithgow be a reverend man of worthie memore, quhilis Maister William of Foulis, archedene of Sanct Andrewis, eftir the tenor of his chartir of fundation made tharupon, as I will ansere in that actione before the heeast Juge. Alsa I obliss me that I sal mak ministracion at my cunning and knawledge in the parisch kirk and in the quere of the said burgh in divine service, sic as afore used dayli and continualy in matutine, mess, evynsang, lladymes, salve, and processione, gif the said baileyheis and counsale thinkis expedient that continuale service be made, and uthirquhiles on festivale dayes and haly dayes, as the caiss requer. And attour I obliss me that I sal kepe and conserve all the graith and reparatione of the said altare, bukis, chalice, chesabill, albis, towallis, and the apparaling of tham to the profet of the said altare. And at I sal not sell, wedset, nor anale ony part of the graith of the said altare, for na mistere may happyn me in ony tyme to cum, and gif I do the contrare in ony thing I renunce my said service, to be quite thereof in al tymes to cum. Alsa I obliss me be thir presents that I sal govern my person in honeste and be of honest conversation in mete and drink, lying and rising, and at I sal not use unressonable excess, nor continual concubine. And gif me happyne to do the contrare, I sal, at the ordinance and consale of the said baileyheis and communitie desist and amend, under payne of deprivacion fra my said service ; and in tymes to cum I sal leyr diligentli to rede and sing in augmentation to Godd's service and for pleasance of the said baileyheis and communitie. And till all thir thingis before writin lelei and treuli to be kepit in manere and fourme, the haly evangell twichit, I have gevyn a bodily aith in presence of the baileyheis and communitie of the said burgh. And for the mare sikernes, I have fundyn thir worthi person borrowis and pleges for me that the said condicione sal be kepit. That is to say, Henry of Livingstone of Middlebenny, Walter of Hamilton, William of Saltone, Thomas of Cowers, William Brone my fadyr, and John Brone my brodir. In witnes of the quilk thing the said persons in takenyng of thare borrowyng has set to thare selis the xxiii day of the moneth of Februare, the yhere of our Lord Iᵐ foure hundir fifti and fyve yheres.

(Seal)   (Seal)   (Seal)   (Seal)   (Seal)   (Seal)

The King wavered long, but his French connections, his aversion to English dictation, and more than all, the claims the Church had on him, at length turned the scale.

To understand the hold the Church had on James V. it is necessary to go into some details of his life. These have been furnished lately in some fulness by the late Dr. G. D. Gib, who wrote *The Life and Times of Robert Gib*, stirrup-man or head groom to James V., and *laird*, not *lord*, of Carribber*—in some respects a very interesting book, although useless for its

---

* Rob's father, according to the Doctor, was stirrup-man to James IV., and was with him at Flodden, and returned alive. Rob succeeded to the office of his father, and by and bye to the small estate of Easter Carribber, which he inherited from his uncle Robert Carribber of that ilk. Rob also owned some land at Kincavel and at Birkenshaw in the Barony of Ogilface. Rob must have been " a man of some substance," as he had the honour of being married to Elizabeth Shaw, the first of the King's avowed mistresses who had a child to him. Descendants of Rob were valets to James VI. The last of them was Sir Henry Gib, who, Dr Gib says, was made a Baronet of Nova Scotia, and who died 1650. His brother, James, however, did not succeed to, or did not claim the title, and sold Carribber. The ruins of the mansion house at Carribber are still known as " Rob Gib's Castle," and are prettily situated above a ravine on the Avon about two miles west from Linlithgow. A carved stone from the ruin, bearing the royal arms, is built into the wall of a cottage near the roadside near bye. Rob must have been a man of some " character "—genial and witty withal, else his name would not have been so familiarly preserved. The only story recorded of him is that told by Scott (who by the way, has transposed it into the reign of James VI.). The King one day made Rob take his place in his own royal chair, and set the courtiers to pay their obeisance and prefer their requests to him. Rob, however, repelled them all " as a set of unmercifully greedy sycophants, who followed their worthy King only to see what they could make of him. ' Get ye hence, ye covetous selfish loons,' he exclaimed, ' and bring to me my own dear and trusty servant Rob Gib, that I may honour the only one of my Court that serves me for stark love and kindness.' " Whether this story be true or not, " ROB GIB'S CONTRACT " became a proverbial saying, and a motto for a " posy ring." " *Rob Gib's contract—stark love and kindness* " occurs, according to Dr Gib, in *Kithy's Collection of Scottish Proverbs, 1721*. A ring with the motto or posy was found near the Palace not very long ago.

purpose of justifying the assumption of a Baronetcy. Rob Gib—the King's fool, as he has been popularly called, was not, at least formally, such. There is, according to Dr Gib, mention in 1530 of Malcom the King's fool, and in 1541 of John Lowise, fool, and of Serat, the Queen's fool; also of John Durche, the King's dwarf, and of another called the Little Turk. The married life of James at Linlithgow would seem to have been much the same as that of his father James IV. Under the curatorship of the Douglases, James's education was neglected, and, as appears from Sir David Lindsay's poems, he was encouraged in vicious indulgence. It was scarcely to be expected, when James came so young to be his own master that he would shake himself clear of this, and the state of European morals was such that he found willing accomplices among his needy nobility. Dr Gib gives the following list of James's grander mistresses and natural children:—

I. By ELIZABETH, daughter of Sir James Shaw of Sauchie, in Stirling, and who afterwards married Robert Gib of Carribber—*Lord James Stewart*, born in 1530 or 1531, constituted Abbot of Kelso and Melrose 1540, died in 1558 without issue.

II. By LADY MARGARET, daughter of John, twelfth Lord Erskine, and who afterwards married Sir Robert Douglas of Lochleven—*Lord James Stewart* (Regent Murray), born in 1533, and in 1540 was constituted Prior of St. Andrews.

III. By ELIZABETH, daughter of Sir John Carmichael, Captain of Crawford, and who afterwards married Sir John Somerville of Camnethan—1. *Lord John Stewart*, who became Prior of Coldingham, and died at Inverness in 1563. 2. *Lady Jean Stewart*, who married Archibald, fifth Earl of Argyle.

IV. By EUPHEMIA, daughter of Alexander, Lord Elphinstone—*Lord Robert Stewart*, Prior of Holyrood.

V. By LADY ELIZABETH STEWART, daughter of John, third Earl of Lennox (who was slain at Linlithgow-Bridge)—*Lord Adam Stewart*, who was made Prior of the Charter-house of Perth.

The consent of the Church to such heavy drafts* as these appointments implied, even although the appropriation of

---

* Such lay appointments to the emoluments of richly endowed religious establishments were nothing new, either here or over Europe. Even so far back as the time of St. Margaret, wife of Malcom Canmore, that much belauded ritualistic lady, zealous reformer of rites and observances as she was, does not seem, according to Mr Skene *(Celtic Scotland)*, to have objected to the endowment of one of her own sons out of Church revenues. She met and argued with the old-style clergy, and so, with Malcom at her back, helped to bring the Scottish ritual into conformity with that of the prevailing party in the Western or Romish Church. The price she thus paid seems to have been held more than sufficient to cover the money draft, for she was in addition raised

Church revenues for similar purposes by the highest clergy was common, was not to be had for nothing. The price seems to have been the King's consent to an active persecution. An inquisition into men's religious opinions commenced in 1534, under the direction of Sir James Hamilton of Finnart. There is allusion in some older writers to a house of the Dominicans in the easter part of the town. The old tower and its surrounding buildings may possibly have been used by them for inquisitorial purposes. Sir James Hamilton, the Sheriff, now fled to England, and many were burnt, and so, apparently, have been the local records of this period. Sir John Borthwick was most probably the next Sheriff of Linlithgow.* Cardinal Beaton succeeded in 1539 to the primacy, and, high in influence with the King, he made use of his position to recommence the persecution of the reformers. In the grand meeting of Bishops and Nobles which he called at St. Andrews, after his appointment as Legate, he denounced some of the principal reformers, and in particular, Sir John Borthwick, as one of the most industrious of them all. Sir John had to flee like his predecessor. He was employed by Henry VIII. in a mission to the Protestant princes of Germany, but returned to his native country to share in the triumph of the Reformation. The state of the King's mind about this time was a most unenviable one, his nature being one for which such work as Beaton, "cruel cardinall," urged him to authorise, was most unfitted. After the execution of Sir James Hamilton of Finnart—who was accused of having conspired against the King's life while he was in the keeping of the Douglases, at Holyrood, by attempting to murder him in bed; and at Linlithgow, by shooting at him from the palace and from the steeple—the King was troubled with frightful visions. One of these is related by Knox in his *History of the Reformation* as occurring here :—

---

to a Saintship. Malcom and his subjects used to be represented as a sort of half savages whom she made it her mission to reclaim. So far as appears from authentic history, they seem to have been quite as civilized as their neighbours, the English.

* He was a son of William, third Lord Borthwick. He is called "Provost of Linlithgow," possibly a misprint for Sheriff, in one account of Cardinal Beaton's denunciation of him. He was captain of the King's French Guard.

How terrible a Vision the said Prince saw lying in *Linlithgow* that Night that *Thomas Scot* Justice-Clerk died in *Edinburgh*, Men of good Credit can yet report : For afraid at Midnight, or after, he called aloud for torches, and raised all that lay beside him in the Palace, and told that *Thomas Scot* was dead ; for he had been at him with a Company of Devils, and had said unto him these Words, *O wo to the Day that ever I knew thee or thy Service ; for serving of thee, against God, against his Servants, and against Justice, I am adjudged to endless Torment.*

Subject to the influences indicated, and with no liking either to burn or to be burnt to maintain the debauchery of kings and priests, there seems little doubt that the people of the place were mostly inclined towards the Reformation; but this is more evident in the affair of the Provostship. It would appear that on the flight of Borthwick, influence was success-fully made with the King to allow the burgesses to elect a Provost, with the powers of Sheriff within burgh, for them-selves. Henry Forrest, through whose influence principally the grant or charter was obtained, was unanimously chosen as the first Provost of the burgh on the 1st day of October 1540. He was re-elected on the 23rd of September 1541, there being eighty-eight burgesses present. This meeting would appear to have been got up as a special demonstration in anticipation of what was to follow, as the meeting does not appear to have proceeded to the usual election of bailies, officers, and council. On the 3rd of October, the usual time for the election, the Queen-Dowager's husband, Lord Methven, Sheriff-principal of the sheriffdom, appears with a missive letter from the King, commanding the bailies, council, and community to appoint a person "abill to be thankfull and appliabill" . . . "twching sic things as may happin to occur" . . . "and that ye remove Henry Forrest now Provost out of the said office." Forrest was accordingly removed, and Robert Wutherspoon was chosen in his place, by an assize of twenty-eight persons " chosin for chusing" him and the other officials. After the election and swearing in of the new council on the 7th, the council (with Sir David Lindsay sitting as a member of it) proceeds to business. Their first Act is significant, as implying some laxity in the community as to Church attendance :—

The said day it is statuted and ordaint be the provost, baillies, and counsale of this burgh of Linlithgw, for the weill fair of this burgh, That thay and all uther honest persones thairof, observe and keep all-soung, evinsang, and mess, in the kirk ; sayand and makand thair devotion to God Almighty and his

Modir the blissit virgin Marie; besekand thame for the common weill of this burgh, whilk be thair grace mot incress.

Other Acts of this worthy council are to the effect, that, in all time coming, the old council should choose the new; that the new council with the deacons of crafts should choose the provost, bailies, and officers; and that no councillor should divulge what passed in council. Alexander Stewart, brother to Lord Methven, appears on the 2nd of October of the year following, 1542, with another letter commanding the council and community to re-elect Robert Wutherspoon, and to choose for bailies and officers "qualifeit substantius persones, and of knawleg."* A third letter of the King's was presented by "Henry Foulis, sheriff in that part"—"chargeand the provost and baillies to obey the samin; whilk thay did after the nateur of the samyn; and the provost and baillies requirit the copy of the said letter." This was presented on the 6th December, and the nature of it can only be conjectured; and dark enough conjectures there were regarding the King's, or more properly the Cardinal's, secret designs at this time: but these, whatever they may have been, were extinguished by the King's death on the 13th of the same month. Forrest re-appears, as we learn only incidentally from one of the Treasurer's annual accounts, as Provost in 1543. There is no doubt that a different construction might be put upon this interference of the King. In 1535 an act was passed ordaining that "no outland man," that is, no man who did not dwell within burgh, should be Provost of a burgh, on account that such persons made use of the office "for thare aine particular weill in consuming the commoun guids." If Forrest was a landed proprietor in the neighbourhood, he might come within the description of an "outland man," but his thorough popularity seems inconsistent with the notion that he used his office in such a way, although it may be insinuated in a phrase contained in the letter delivered by Alexander Stewart—"to performing thair offices sua that of necessitie thay sall not uss the comon gud to thair awn particular offecis." If—recollecting who was the King's right

---

* The pretexts of absolutism are ever the same. An Act of Parliament of 1469, in the minority of James III., is to the same effect, that the old councils should choose the new, "on account of great trouble and contention yearly by common simple persons."

hand man at this time—for "offices" we read "opinions" it probably represents the true state of matters.

It may be necessary to explain that the community of the Burgh had the charge of the Church, both as to the appointment of the chaplains or priests, who were often the sons of townsmen; and as to the upholding of the fabric. The patronage of some of the altarages was however retained by the founders. It was usual that the clergy upheld the choir, but practically the whole building came under the management of the Town Council. The Priory of St. Andrews, which was superior of most of the houses on the north side of the street east from the Cross, and held these as part of their Regality on this side of the Forth, compounded with the community for an annual payment of 205 merks for the upholding of the choir. The original indenture of this or some other such agreement exists, in a sorely dilapidated state, in the town's possession. The Council drew, also, the "Procraftis of the kyrk," being the sums payable by the Crafts or Trades for maintaining their altars, and the fines of the craftsmen—at least these do not appear under any other heading; Legacies, Lare Siller [grave dues], and Church-offerings. Some of the altarages were richly endowed with "annual rents" payable out of various lands and tenements, to the number (including those payable for the maintenance of the lights or wax tapers used on St. Michael's or the High altar, and at the celebration of the Sacrament or High Mass) of 228. There is evidence in the Court-book, from records of infeftments taken by the priests on lands and tenements, and other notices, that there were, at the least, thirteen chaplains or priests in the church, and there may have been even a greater number. Besides the High Altar, there were the following :—

Sancte Trinitatis—(of the Holy Trinity)

Sancte Crucis—(of the Holy Cross, or Rood)

Corporis Christi—(of the Body of Christ)—founded by William of Foulis, Archdeacon of St. Andrews.

Sancti Cruoris—(of the Holy Blood)

Sancte Beate Marie Virginis—("Our Lady" altar)

Sancti Salvatoris—(of the Holy Saviour, or St. Saviour's)

Sancti Johannis Baptiste—(of St. John the Baptist)

Sancti Johannis Evangeliste—(of St. John the Evangelist)

Sancti Petri—(St. Peter's)

Sancti Andree—(St. Andrew's)

Sancte Beate Marie Virginis—(of the Blessed Mary.   The other altar to Mary
    was founded by the burgh ; this and the next two by Robert Begys.)

Sancte Brigide—(St. Bryde's)

Sancte Anne—(St. Anne's)

Sancte Katherine Virginis—(St. Katherine's)

Sancti Niniani—(St. Ninian's)

Sancti Eligii—(of St. Eloy, the patron saint of the Hammermen.   St. Eloy had
    been a Goldsmith, and hence came it that it was " a lady's oath—By
    Saint Eloy "

Sanctorum Crispinii et Crispiniani—(St. Crispins')

Sancti Stephani—(St. Stephen's—these two were upheld by the Shoemakers)

Sancti Cutberti—(St. Cuthbert's—upheld by the Coopers)

Sancti Nicholai—(St. Nicholas')

Sancte Sithe—(St. Syth's)

Sancti Antionii—(St. Anthony's)

Omnium Sanctorum—(All-Saints')

Twenty-four in all, so far as can be learned; and there may
have been more, as it is only from solitary and incidental
notices that several of these have been ascertained. With at
least thirteen priests in the church, and possibly as many
friars in the friary, the town must have been sufficiently
priest-ridden.

As already noticed, the town's early records have been
mostly lost or destroyed, but the Court-book contains some
record of the " Kyrk werk " in the reign of James.V. There
are preserved agreements with Patrick Franch in 1528; with
Thomas in 1530 and 1532. The last of these runs as follows:—

Decimo-sexto die menis Maii, Anno Domini, M. Vmo. XXXII.

Quo die, Thomas Franch maister masoune, obliss hime be the faith and treuth
off his body, to the bailzies, counsale, and communitie of Linlithgw that he
sall leiff his twa sonnes to werk at the kyrk werk of Lithgw, to the endyne
of the gavill of the stane werk with a courss of the batallyne round about.
And the said Thomas sall cum within a xiiij dais eftir Whitsunday to the
kyrk werk of Lithgw, and sall byde with thame ane xiiij dais to the endyne
of the kyrk werk.   And alsua the said Thomas maister masoune sall be payt
his fie for the xiiij dais that he is away, and for the xiiij dais that he cumis
and werks, with his sonnes payment to be payt sic like as thay had forrow,
and xxs to be gene to thame for thair drynk silvyr.   Subscribit with the said
Thomas Franchis hand, day, zear, moneth, and plass, forsaid.

THOMAS FRANCH, manu propria.

There are also references to "Sanct Michaelis werk" as in progress, at least as regards the wood work, in 1536. This piece of work was in all probability the three-sided apse with the three tall windows after the "perpendicular" fashion. The centre arch dividing the choir from the nave was removed when the eastern part of the church was fitted up as the Parish Church about sixty-five years ago, and the crown was removed eight years after, from an apprehension that it would tumble down. In the choir aisles the lines of the groining are round masses of foliage encircling shields. In the north aisle those decipherable are a Fleur-de-lis, the Cross and Crown, and a Heart and Hands—the two latter well-known emblems. In the south, the only one left is the Scottish lion on a crowned shield. In the nave the bosses are seal-shaped, and the shields are enclosed in rings, the only two of which that are decipherable are the three cinquefoils of the Hamiltons, and three crescents within a bordure of roses, the arms probably of the Melvilles of Railt and Murdocairney, who seem to have had some connection with Linlithgow and the Court, as Sir Robert Melville, afterwards Lord Melville, was appointed keeper of the palace in 1566–67. The transepts bear the Arms of the Burgh. The dimensions of the building over all externally are about 187 by 105 feet; internally, 180, or, excluding the steeple and apse, 146 feet long by 62 in breadth, excluding the transepts.

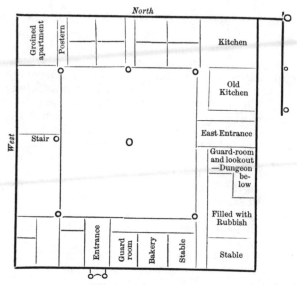

General Plan of Ground Floor of Palace.

CHAPTER VI.

THE TWO MARYS, REGENT MURRAY, AND JAMES VI.

IT is very difficult to say whether Linlithgow, which, hitherto, had ranked as one of the "worthy and principal towns," had decreased in absolute wealth and population, though it very likely had in comparative consequence, previous to this time; but it is certain that it emerged from the troubles of the Reformation era in a poor plight in both respects. For this we have the testimony of King James VI., who describes it in one of his charters as having "fallen off very much," and as having been "formerly one of the principal Burghs of the kingdom."

After the death of James V., the place of the infant Queen's residence was fixed by Parliament to be either in the Palace here or at Stirling, as the Queen-Dowager might prefer ; and she accordingly remained here for a few months, until Beaton and his party, with a force of ten thousand men, carried off the Queen and her mother to Stirling. Beaton had been defeated in his attempt to seize the regency, and had been confined in Blackness castle in the beginning of the year, and he had now his revenge on the Hamiltons and their supporters, who mustered strong in the town and neighbourhood. Sir David Lindsay, in his "Tragedie of the Cardinall," makes Beaton relate the story :—

> The governour purposing to subdew,
> I raisit ane oyst of mony bald barroun,
> And maid ane raid, whilk Lithgow yet may rew ;
> For we destroyit ane myle about the toun,
> For that I got mony black malisoun :
> Yet, contrair the governouris intent,
> With our young princess, we to Striveling went.

In 1544, the rough wooing of Henry VIII., who sent a fleet into the Firth of Forth with an army, compelled Beaton and Arran, who were now reconciled, to retreat hither from Edinburgh with Huntly, Argyle, and the rest of the lords; and in the following year they held meetings of Parliament in the Palace in September, October, and December. It was this Parliament, according to the *Diurnal of Occurrents*, to which the nobles flocked "for land," that is, for a share of the forfeited lands. Beaton was not long in power till he recommenced a persecution of the reformers, which was carried on until he was himself murdered in his own castle of St. Andrews in 1546. Of the doings in the busy years that follow till 1559,—the war with England, and the contests of the Reformers with the Queen Regent supported by her party and her French auxiliaries,—there is of local interest on record, the holding of a Provincial Council here in 1552 for the purpose of devising measures to appease the popular outcry against the clergy; and the burning of the shipping at Blackness, by Lord Clynton, Admiral of the English fleet. There is a letter with the signature of the Queen Regent of date 1557, preserved in the Charter-chest, exempting the burgh from sending their quota of men to the army at Fala-

muir, for payment of £100—one of the schemes for raising
money sometimes adopted by the princes of the time; and
there is one solitary act or decision of the Burgh-court, which
has been carefully preserved and printed, as a sort of fishers'
charter :—

> *Curia Burgi de Linlichtgow, tenta ibidem coram Jacobo Denniston præposito,*
> *Jacobo Rae et Magistro Bartholomew Kellie, Ballivis ejusdem nono die*
> *mensis Septembris Anno Domini 1552.*

NOMINA ASSIZE—Robt. Wetherspone, Henry Forrest, Peter Newlands, Rob.
Ross, William Knolles, Alexr. Roust, John Thomson, Robert Jamie,
William Eliston, Rob. Reddine, John Gibbiesone.

THE quhilk day comperit in judgement, Thomas Smyth, and persuit and
followit Simon Callrigg, Robert Johnstone, John Henderson, John Loure,
Als. Perkie, Willie Stakks, John Gibson, Allan Bishop,

For the wronguse fishing of the locht of Linlightgow, pertaining to him in
tack and assedation, as he alleadged.

Quhilks persons present deneyed the wrang; therefore alleadgand the same
hes bein in use, that the inhabitants within this brugh hes fishin the louch
past memory of men, without stop, soe fare as they might wade with ane guad,
and submitted them to the knowledge of the foresaid Assize.

Quhilk furth of [court] removant, in returnand again be the fore speaker
Henrie Forrest Chancellar thereof, fand and determinit all in ane voice, that
the saids persons hes done nae wrang in the fishing of the said louch, because
it hes bein in use that the inhabitants within the said burgh hes fishit the said
louch in all time by past, sae fare as they might waid with ane guad; and
therefor exoners them of the said wrang.

It was in 1558 that the reforming lords separated themselves from the Romish Church and took the name of the
Lords of the Congregation. In 1559 they took their famous
march from Perth, destroying monasteries and friaries, and
clearing away the altars and images from the churches. It
was on the 29th of June they passed through here. The only
image they have spared about the church is that of St. Michael,
which yet faces to the Kirkgate. A statue of a saint is still
occasionally found in the floor of a cellar in the town, and a
bit of an altar-piece in rude bas-relief is preserved in one of
the transepts of the Church. It was got inside of the Church,
when digging a grave; and, from the style of the sculpture
and ornament, is probably more ancient than the present
edifice. Some of the panels of the old stone pulpit which was
attached to one of the great pillars at the east end of the
nave are still preserved below the altar-piece. The pulpit
was removed when the church was last repaired. The friary
seems to have been entirely demolished by the Reformers, if

not already decayed, as it appears, by a lease of their lands in 1545, that a prior and three brethren were then the whole of the body. The foundations of a house, at Friarbank, were lately come upon, supposed to have been the Friary.

On the 6th November, in consequence of their defeat by the Queen's French forces from Leith, the Lords of the Congregation had to retreat from Edinburgh to this place, where "they remained in consultation and preparing for the wars, and will set up a coin, saying they shall coyne a good part of their plate for maintenance of the word of God, and the wealth of Scotland."* One of the traditions regarding the Square Tower near the railway station, is, that it was "the mint of Scotland," and it is quite possible that it may have been used for the purpose of a mint at this time. The French troops were here in March following, and on the way back from Glasgow "ran the foray about be the space of sax myles, and brocht in all the cattle, horss, and uther geir that mycht be gottin thair, to the great destruction of the country."† The Lords of the Congregation triumphed, however, and the "Reformation Parliament," as it is called, was held in Edinburgh, in 1560.

Queen Mary arrived from France in the year following. There is little trace of her residence in the Palace farther than in passing visits. It was on one of these occasions she was met on the way to Edinburgh, and carried off by Bothwell. The Lords were up again in array against the Queen, and the Hamiltons were advancing to her aid, and had arrived here when the news of the defeat at Carbery reached them. The only other event in the history of Mary, in connection with the neighbourhood, was her first halt, after her escape from Lochleven castle, at Niddry, a square tower, then belonging to the Setons, of which the traveller from Edinburgh by the railway catches a glimpse, to his right hand, before entering the tunnel at Winchburgh, six miles east from Linlithgow.

Of the very few acts of the Burgh-court preserved, one in 1564, when order was thought to have been restored, is very significant—"that thair actis in all time cuming be deullie observit, preservit, and not dispensand with the same by the

---

* *Intelligence from Scotland.*—Appendix to Tytler's History.
† *Diurnal of Occurrents.*

aviss of the haill counsall." Order does not seem to have prevailed very long, however, as the court is found, shortly after, ordering the town to be kept, night and day, by watch and ward. In 1565 they are found arranging for the slating of the church, which had been previously covered with lead—a considerable portion of the lead having probably been taken away for the manufacture of bullets. There are some appointments of persons to draw the revenues of altars, so as to secure these for the common good, by redispositions. These proceedings are confirmed by the charter of James VI. of 1591; and Ludovic, Earl of Lennox, Commendator of St. Andrews, and Lord St. John, are found in other documents disponing the annual-rents due to the priory and the preceptory, as well as their Bailleries within burgh, to the community. The annual-rents payable to the altars were in some cases, if not in all, redisponed by the community to the owners of lands and tenements out of which they were payable. To one of these charters, of date 1598, the old great seal of the burgh is still appended. The seal differs slightly from the present great seal, the side on which St. Michael appears being more elegant, and the other side less so. The Burgh-mills came also into the burgh's possession in 1560, by disposition of Jean Livingston, the last prioress of Manuel convent. Dame Jeane and Dame Margaret Cokburne sign this deed, each "with my hand at the pen led by the notar."

Ninian Winzet, the schoolmaster of the burgh for the ten years from 1551 till 1561, deserves mention. He seems to have been much aggrieved by his dismissal from the grammar school of "that my kyndly toun;" and he blames the preacher "Dene Patrik Kinloquhy," and the Superintendent of the district, Spottiswood, for his dismissal. He appears to have been a conscientious adherent of the Romish church, and a clever man, fond of argumentation. He devoted himself afterwards to publishing controversial tracts, some of them addressed to John Knox, but had very soon to leave the country, and he ultimately got the appointment of Abbot of St. James's, the Scots convent, at Ratisbon.*

After the battle of Langside, the houses of the Hamiltons

---

* See Irving's *Lives of Scottish Writers.*

were plundered, and thirteen carts laden with valuables and furniture, from Hamilton, Draffen, and Kinneil, passed through to Edinburgh; some of the bulky articles being sold by the way at the Cross. The vigorous rule of "the good Regent," Murray, seemed to render the success of the opposite, or Queen's party, hopeless, and several attempts at his assassination were made, the last of which proved successful. John Hamilton of Bothwellhaugh was the instrument of the Queen's party on this occasion.* The Regent was proceeding with an armed force from Stirling to Edinburgh, and lodged here on the night of the 19th January 1570. One of the roads to Edinburgh was by way of Mid-Calder, and it left Linlithgow by what is called the Dog-well wynd, and it would appear that the Regent was going by it. Hamilton concealed himself in the house of his uncle, Archbishop Hamilton, which stood next west to that of Charles Drummond of Riccarton, then Provost of the town. From the gallery of the house, Hamilton fired at the Regent, the ball passing through his belly and killing the horse of Arthur Douglas who rode beside him. Hamilton, who had a swift horse ready, succeeded in making his escape. The Regent died in the Palace at eleven o'clock, on the night of the 20th. The house from which the Regent was shot, according to the *Diurnal,* "incontinent thairefter wes all utterlie burnt with fyre."

The County-Court buildings and the Prison now occupy the ground where "Riccarton's lodging," as Drummond's house was for long called, and that of the Archbishop stood. A bronze portrait tablet has lately been inserted in the wall of the Court-house as a sort of sign-post to visitors—some of the contributors carefully guarding themselves against the idea of their contributing towards erecting anything in honour of the Regent. The design is by Sir Noel Paton, and it has been beautifully modelled by his sister, Mrs D. O. Hill. The exact spot where the Regent fell is almost directly opposite the north-west corner of the building. When the old buildings

---

* A mythical story used to do duty as exonerating the Queen's party from complicity in the assassination, and as an excuse or justification for Hamilton. It is that Sir John Bellenden, Justice-Clerk, got a grant of the forfeited lands of Woodhouselee, and had turned out Hamilton's wife naked on a cold winter night among the Pentland hills, where she went mad !

on the site were taken down, Hamilton's house revealed in its
eastern part, which had been turned into a two-storey dwelling house, a fine large hall with a round arch at the east end,
somewhat like that in the large hall of the Palace. A coat-of-
arms from Riccarton's lodging is preserved in one of the gables
of the prison. It bears date, however, of 1647.

Linlithgow seems to have been the head-quarters of the
Queen's party about this time, and it suffered in consequence;
Lennox and the English army, in revenge of the Regent's
death, burning the houses of the Queen's adherents in the
town and neighbourhood—Pardovan, Binny, Kincavel, Niddry,
Livingston, and Kinneil—scarce leaving them a stone house
habitable. When the English troops left the country, they
carried off with them to Berwick, Charles Drummond, as well
as the Provost of Haddington, because they would not give
pledges to prevent the assembling of the Hamiltons and their
party in their respective towns. The towns were neither large
nor properly walled, so that it would have been impossible for
them to have made such pledges good.

Blackness Castle in the succeeding few years changed hands
several times. Alexander Stewart, the Governor, betrayed it
to Queen Mary's party for 800 crowns, because as he said "the
Regent and the King's Lords would not give him anything to
keep it with." The most romantic story in connection with
it is the betrayal of Sir James Kirkaldy by his wife, in 1573,
to the Regent Morton. Sir James returning from France
with 50,000 double-ducats—arrears of the Queen's dowry—to
help the cause, and landing at Blackness, had been made
prisoner by the keeper of the castle, who, in the absence of
Sir James, had gone over to the other side. While in prison
Sir James managed to gain over the men, and kept the castle.
His wife came to visit him, and induced him to accompany
her for a short way when leaving, when he was seized by
Captain Lambie, at this time keeper of Linlithgow Palace, and
sent next day to Edinburgh. He shortly after made his
escape, and on the eighth morning thereafter his wife was
found lying strangled in her bedroom! As some accounts
endow Blackness about this time with fabulous docks and
quays, another story regarding it may not be out of place. It
is from the Burgh-court book :—

" *1540, 17. January.* Comperit Charles Denniston, captane of the hous and strength of Blakness, under our Soveraine lord, the Kingis Grace, and hevely meanit and complenit upon the Baillies of the Burgh forsaid, That tha suld have rasit ane havy and aggravouss slander upone him, sayand he suld injurouslie have skatitt, tollit, and wrangouslie tane certane hundirs herying fra fyve bots or thairby that came to the said Blakness pier with herying."

The bailies, after clearing themselves, discovered the real offender in John Barbour, who was condemned to sit down in the court on his knees and say " *Tongue, ye lied;*" and to repeat the same performance at the Cross on the next market-day.

With James VI. the Palace seems to have been a favourite held here in 1585, 1593, and 1596. He seems to have made some alterations on the west side, the large window in what is called Queen Mary's room, and bearing his initials, having been opened or enlarged by him, as well, possibly, as the upper small windows in the same apartment. The somewhat uncommon long narrow window lighting up the ceiling of the adjoining chamber may also have been his work. It would appear that in the midst of the confusion of the strife between King's men and Queen's men, the preservation of the royal retirement. Three of his Parliaments or Conventions were property had been comparatively neglected, and the dwellers near the loch had been encroaching—hence the following letter to the magistrates :—

REX. Provost and baillies of our burgh of Linlytgow we grete you weill Fforsamekill as we and our predecessors hes bein accustomat to have our horses wateritt besyde our Paleice be the watter yett in the Kirkgait be ane ampill passage swa that they mycht pace and repace by utheris without impediment, Nochtwtstanding being informit That sum inhabitantis in that our burgh pretenand richt to the tenementis and ruids adjacent to our said loch his not onlie stoppit the passage of our saids horses be including the samyn be dyikis Bot also in the late drouths of somer extendit the bounds and limitis of thair tenementis far within owr said loch to the grait preiudice of our orchardis and yeardis adjacent to our said Paleice be staying the samin to flow owr the auld bounds theirof and causing the samyn in respect of your restreayning to owrflow our Peill and orchardis of our said Paleice Geving us thairby to mervell of you, yeur slothfullnes thairin and owrsicht in staying thame, Quha altogidar sould have Respectit us In that behalf. It is thairfor our will and we expreslie comand you That upone the sicht heirof ye stay all fardir building of the samyn dyikis and destroy and cast downe all that ar allreddie biggit within the bounds of the flowing of our said Loch except that dyik biggit be Nicholl Bell ffor restreayning of the passage frome our said Peill, as ye and ilk ane of you will answer to us upon your officeis and obedience and will discharge yourself theirof Whairanent thir presentis sall be your warrand Sub-

scribit with our hand at our Castell of Sterling the xvii day of August 1599
Sic subscrib.   JAMES R.*

In another letter the King complains of the same grievance as
hindering the washing of his horses, as well as obstructing the
inhabitants from passing along the shore of the loch for the
purpose of washing their clothes ; and he commands the magistrates to hinder all encroachment beyond what was wont to be
cultivated, "notwithstanding of whatsumevir letters purchest
or to be purchest at our hand." It would appear, further, that
the inhabitants had been in the habit, before Nicol Bell's dyke
was built (at the Vennel, it may be presumed), of bleaching
their clothes in the Peel.

The Livingstons, who had been favourites with Mary of
Guise, and one of whom was selected as one of the four Marys
who were to be the companions of their little mistress, Queen
Mary, were also favourites with James VI., who in 1600 conferred the title of Earl of Linlithgow upon Alexander, Lord
Livingston. His Lordship was one of the nobles to whom
the education of the Princes and Princesses was committed—
the Princess Elizabeth, who afterwards married the King of
Bohemia, being consigned to his care. The great Palace of

---

* The whole of the land in and around the town and loch appears to have
been at one time royal property. These possessions were considerably dimin-
ished by the time of James VI., but still included most of the land in the immediate vicinity of the Palace. The following is a translation of part of an
Act of Parliament fixing the dowry of the Queen of James II., of which the
Palace and lands here formed part :—" Our Mansion or Palace beside the loch,
with the Loch and fishings of the same ; and all and whole the Great-Customs
and Burgh-Rent of our Burgh of Linlithgow, with the office of Sheriff of the
same ; and all and whole our Lands under-written, to wit :—Kyncavil, Drum-
cross ; all and whole our acres at the east and west ends of said Burgh, with
the Sanctuary crofts, Bonytone, the Lochside, Kyngsffelde, with the annual
rents of the Orchard croft, and of the Fethel-croft."

FETHEL CROFT.—The name of this piece of the royal grounds, after passing
through the intermediate stage of " Fidilcroft," has now been changed into
" the Fiddler's Croft." This was probably the croft or piece of land for growing Broom, once rather an important article of food for cattle. The actual
" keepers " of the Palace and grounds, long ago, were usually inhabitants of
the town, and their payment appears, from the notes in the *Spottiswoode Miscellany*, to have been £50 a year. For this they were bound to keep the
grounds, gardens, orchards, &c., in order, and, as appears in the grant to
Andrew Ferrier (1567), they were commanded and charged " to labour and
manure certain faulds of brume within the said Pealis [grounds], for holding
and pasturing of our souveraines meiris thairintill." The word is probably
the old English *Battil* or *betle*, " fertile," allied to the old Norse *beit*, a pasture.

Hiedelberg, which was the future residence of this princess, is said to have been indebted to her for the marked resemblance it is said to bear to the palace here.

The accession of James to the throne of England, in 1603, closed in great measure the connection of Linlithgow with royalty; and the Earl of Linlithgow appears to have been left occupant of the Palace. The north side which for two years previous had been in a perilous state, "fell in," leaving the walls standing, between three and four of the morning of 6th September 1607; and the inner wall threatened to fall, also, and to destroy the fountain.* The Palace must have been in this condition at the date of the King's visit to Scotland in 1617; when he gave orders for the rebuilding of the north side. It is a pity that, so far as known, nothing has been preserved to indicate the style of the older building. The design for the rebuilding would of course be made by the King's "Master Mason" or Architect for Scotland for the time being—probably by William Wallace, who eight years afterwards designed Heriot's Hospital in Edinburgh. Before the original records were examined, and writers went by conjecture, all such buildings of this time used to be ascribed to Inigo Jones, the Queen's Architect in London, who designed Whitehall. There are architectural features peculiarly Scotch in the Palace here, and in Heriot's Hospital, which could scarcely have occurred to Mr Jones.

The grand entrance to the Lyon Chamber recently re-opened seems to have been shut up at this time. Whether the apartment in the north corner on the level of the Lyon Chamber was at this time converted into a kitchen is doubtful, but the vaulted roof, either now or at some former time, has been removed to lighten the walls. The springings of the arches of the groining are worth attention, they being different from anything else here of that kind. There is a similar kitchen in the vaulted apartment below, communicating with the Lyon Chamber by a passage and spiral staircase. The fire-places of neither have been part of the original design. The fine fountain in the centre of the court must have been partially injured by this time, as one of the lower

---

* *Spottiswoode Miscellany.*

F

balance turrets has been then replaced by one in a different style, out of keeping with the others, and with ornament of the time of James VI., as pointed out by the late Dr Joseph Robertson. Such fountains were meant for dipping out of, and they may still be seen in use in continental towns. The ideas and spirit of the old architecture were lost, and the architect here seems to have thought that the fountain would harmonise better with his new building if raised on a pedestal. The Cross Well of the town has, also, been altered in this way to a much greater extent. The Cross Well has been rebuilt in 1628, in 1659, and in 1807. The alterations of the gothic character of the balance turrets would probably be made in 1628. The top part of the grand fountain erected some time ago at Holyrood is mainly copied from the Palace fountain here.

The inhabitants of the burgh of course got up a great display on the occasion of the King's visit, the most notable part of which was the salutation at the gate, by the schoolmaster of the burgh, who, from the interior of a plaster figure, delivered to his majesty an address commencing :—

> " Thrice royal sir, here do I you beseech,
> Who art a lion, to hear a lion's speech ;
> A miracle ! for since the days of Æsop,
> No lion, till those days, a voice dared raise up
> To such a majesty ! Then, King of men,
> The King of beasts speaks to thee from his den,
> Who, though he now enclosed be in plaster,
> When he was free, was Lithgow's wise schoolmaster."

It was the last time that the authorities had the opportunity of welcoming a resident Sovereign— Whitehall and St. James's, Windsor and Hampton Court, were hereafter to be to the thrice-royal Sirs in the place of Holyrood and Stirling, Falkland and Linlithgow.

Burgh Seal.

CHAPTER VII.

THE COVENANTS, THE RESTORATION, AND
THE REVOLUTION.

THE Reformation was now accomplished, but all the questions raised in the course of the struggle had not been disposed of; and another hundred years or more of intermittent turmoil had to pass before these could be practically settled. Few of the important events of the period occurred in Linlithgow, but much may be learned from its records illustrative of the life and spirit of the time; and in its old character of an advanced post for an invading force, as well as from its position on the great highway to the north and west, a more than ordinary share of incident will be found connected with its history.

It may be necessary to remind the reader that the first "National Covenant" was subscribed in 1579,—in which the King, nobility, and people, bound themselves to maintain the reformed church against all enemies. The three powers in the state were at this time virtually the King, the Nobility, and the Church; and of these three the Church, as the representative of the great body of the people, from the uncompro-

mising character of its leaders and the stern independence of
its principles, was perhaps the most powerful, or at least the
most unmanageable by the King. The clergy maintained
their right of animadverting in the pulpit on public affairs as
a spiritual privilege, and the King had adopted the theory of
the right of kings to govern everything, civil and spiritual,—
their responsibility being to the divinity alone, by whom the
right was conferred. Collisions between the two powers were
inevitable, and Blackness castle found many occupants for its
cells ; and it was in consequence of the rising and tumult at
Edinburgh, on one of these occasions, in 1596, that the Court,
the Privy Council, and the Court of Session, were removed to
what James is said to have designated as his " faithful town
of Linlithgow." Away from the influence of the Edinburgh
populace, it was here, too, that the trial of John Welsh and
the other ministers was conducted before the High Court of
Justiciary in 1604, for treason, as ringleaders of the Aberdeen
Assembly, which had met in defiance of the King's command.
Welsh and the others had been confined for a length of time
previously in Blackness, and they were sentenced to depart
for life from the country as traitors.* Assemblies, in which
the King carried matters his own way, were held here in 1606
and 1608, and a partial episcopacy—the substitution of which
for the combined and powerful action of the presbyterial
church courts, the King so much desired—established.

At his visit to Scotland in 1633, Charles I. in his progress
called at his ancestral palace, and the Town Council seem to
have been at a loss as to how the King's retinue were to be
maintained " seeing the puir peipill hes not wharupon to sus-

---

* Welsh was defended on this occasion, when every one else it is said was
afraid to oppose the King, by Thomas Hope, afterwards the celebrated Sir
Thomas, but then a young man. Welsh is said to have thanked him in court
for his exertions, and said that he felt assured that Hope's posterity would
rise to the highest honours in the place where they now were, while the
posterity of the Chancellor of the Jury, Stewart of Craigie, who had shown
himself inimical to the prisoners, would cease out of the land. Welsh's
alleged benediction or prophecy has been fully realised, the various descendants of Sir Thomas Hope being now the principal landholders in the County.
The first of the Hopes who appears in public life is " Edward Houp," a successful trader or merchant in Edinburgh. He was one of the three Commissioners for Edinburgh in the first General Assembly of the Kirk in 1560, his
fellow Commissioners being John Knox and James Barone.

tain thame." Besides the securing of provisions and lodgings, preparations were made to present a respectable front to his majesty. A house in the Kirkgate being "theikit with straw" the Council order its owner to cover it with slates, "as it was unseemly and a disgrace to the toun;" John Ritchie, mason in Edinburgh, who had done himself so much credit in rebuilding the Cross-well, was sent for "to make ane unicorn for the head of the Market Cross;" several of the Council were to be provided with silk clothes "for the credit of the countre and the towne;" a "fuitt mantell" was borrowed from Edinburgh; and last, not least,

"*June 7*. The quhilk day, In respect that his Majestie is to come to this brugh, And considering how undecent it is to weir plaidis and blew bannetis, Thairfor it is statuitt and ordanit That no person athir in burgh or landwart weir ony banneteis nor plaidis during his Majesties remaining in this his ancient kingdome; And that none resort in the towne with bannettis or plaidis, under the paine of confiscation of thair plaidis and bannettis, and punichment of thair personne."

The "blue bonnets" had their revenge by-and-bye. The idea of divine right, taken up by the father, was held with a still firmer faith by the son, and his dislike of presbyterianism was still stronger. The attempt of Charles to enforce the use of the Liturgy was met in the first instance by the discharge of Jenny Geddes's stool at the head of the clergyman, and shortly after by the determined combination of all who feared the destruction of civil liberty or of Presbyterian government in the Church. And now came the renewal of the Covenant, and the famous Glasgow Assembly of 1638, and raising of armed men to go to the borders for defence of "the guid cause." The quota of men liable for service in the burgh appears by a list in the Minute-book to have been 186, of whom about 40·were drafted at a time. A summary mode of raising money seems to have been put in practice on one occasion, "all persons in the town" being summoned before the Council to declare upon oath what money they had beside them. During the time the people were subscribing the Covenant and forming their plans in Edinburgh, in 1637, the Privy Council and the Courts were removed to Linlithgow once more, but found, one account says, the Palace so much out of repair and the houses in the town so mean that they adjourned to Stirling. Probably they thought themselves too near to Edinburgh, as they are twice found, shortly after, sitting at Linlithgow " watching events."

In the local records of the few succeeding years, there is little worthy of special notice until the expedition of Montrose in 1644, when the town submitted to the Master of Napier after the battle of Kilsyth. Napier was sent here to relieve his father, Lord Napier, now an old man, and other prisoners kept in durance here and in Blackness castle, and to proclaim a meeting of Parliament. The magistrates were afterwards called to account for this submission, and their plea in excuse appears, as well it might, considering the character of Montrose's troops, to have been satisfactory. They set forth—

" That the inhabitants had almost all then fled the town, and the Provost and some of the Bailies were also in the act of retreating, but they were hindered by the women desiring them for God's sake not to leave them in such extremity in danger of the enemy ; And that the Provost and Bailies had been thus constrained to remain ; and to prevent the enemy from burning the toun and killing of all therein, they were compelled to comply with the enemy ; and beseeching them to pardon their weakness."

It is told that after the defeat of Montrose at Philiphaugh, all the Irish (that is, Erse, or gaelic-speaking—Highlanders in fact), men, women, and children, of his following, who could be got hold of, were slaughtered, and that a number of stragglers picked up by Leslie's army on their way to Glasgow, were thrown over Linlithgow-bridge and drowned. If this occurred at Linlithgow-bridge, it is curious that there is no local tradition of it.

The plague which was scourging Edinburgh in 1645 and 1646, obliged the University to remove and hold its classes here for a few months. They were accommodated in the Church, which was boarded off into class-rooms. A meeting of Parliament also was held, for the last time in the Palace, in 1646. A note of expenses incurred by the Burgh Commissioner to the next Parliament is curious :—

The baillie James Gibbison's compt in attending the parl. qlk satt doune 3 November 1646 and rois the 27 March 1647 his dayis attendance with Rot Bell consisting this time of 41 dayis at 40s. per diem .   82 0 0

For my hors hyer all this tyme and the extraordinars   .   25 0 8

Extraordinars with the Agent and severall of the burrows .   .   3 6 0

For two pund the best tobacco that culd be had to gift to the Lord Register at the Provost desir 4 0 0

                                                            ─────────
                                                            114 6 8

The period extending from 1638—"the second Reformation," as it is called—till the Restoration, or at least till the
time of Cromwell's rule, is often looked back upon by Presbyterians as a sort of model time, in which religion flourished
both to an extent which might truly be called national, and
in great purity. The civil authorities were at the call of the
Church courts, ready to support their findings by fine, or
imprisonment, or banishment, as the case might require—
new presbyter was but old priest, as Milton has it; and it is
easy to believe that great external decorum at least prevailed.
The following excerpts from the minutes of Kirk-Session may
shew the extent to which the surveillance of the community
was carried:—

1647, May 2. Ordainis the Bailie thatt visits on the Sabbothe in the foir-
noone, and lykways the elder who visits in the afternoone, to accompanny the
Minister throughe the toune in the eftirnoone efter sermone, everie Sabbothe,
for taking notice who ar att familie exercise, or catechizing, reiding, or the
lyk exercise beseiming the Sabbothe; And who ar not, thatt they according
to thair fault may be punishd.

Ordainis that, upon the Sabbothe, none be sein upon the streat till sex
hours att night without ane lawfull occasion, otherwayes to be punisht as a
Sabboth breaker.

After his victory at Dunbar, Cromwell found, on his advance
towards Stirling, a garrison of forty men in the Palace, which
he fortified to some extent, demolishing for this purpose the
Town-house and other houses in the Kirkgate. The fortification seems to have consisted in enclosing with walls, the
ruins of which remained till within the last forty years, the
space between the exterior gateway and the south front of the
Palace—the Church, which furnished accommodation for his
horses, serving to complete the enclosure. Blackness castle
surrendered, after a short siege, in April 1651; Lord Ochiltree,
who had lain prisoner here since 1631, was one of the prisoners
released by Cromwell's government after the battle of Worcester. If we may believe *Nicoll's Diary*, it was on 3rd April
1652, "blawne up with a powder trayne. *It was reported
that the devill was visiblie seen upon the walls of it at its
up-blowing*,"—so congenial to the devil, in popular estimation,
had been the work that had gone on in its "dungeon and
reching tower." Cromwell does not appear to have made any
lengthened stay, though some of his letters are dated from

Linlithgow, and he is found for a few days in the neighbourhood about the time of the battle of Inverkeithing.* The
garrison appear to have lived on friendly terms with the
inhabitants, and to have been rather fond of ale, as the
Governor is found, in 1652, desiring the Council to limit the
number of "brewsters," in consequence of the disorders of his
soldiers.

The principal councillors of the town fled, on the approach
of Cromwell, to Culross, and did not return till after the
battle of Worcester, when the prospects of the Royalists were
for the time ruined. The Burgh Records had a narrow escape,
Colonel Sanderson sending the Councillors word that if not
ransomed for £100 he would burn them. After supplication
to the commission of the Kirk, then sitting at Stirling, who
promised "that it sould nevir be holdin heireftir as comply-
ance," they succeeded in getting possession for £30, sterling.
The records were immediately sent to Dundee, but after the
storming of that place by General Monk, they had again to
be ransomed by a payment of 48 pounds, Scots, to Lieutenant
Kilpatrick. The "writs" had been mixed up with those of
Dundee, but were separated and brought home, "at the least
so mony as war preservat."

The congregation of the place, now broken up into two
bodies of Resolutioners and Protesters, had of course to seek
accommodation elsewhere—one of them in a barn, until 1656,
when the Governor allowed them to resume occupation of the
Church, the Resolutioners in the east end, and "the pretendit
Session," or Protesters, "whom we suppose," say the others,
"will not professe themselves to be a Sessione of the Supreme
Judicatories of the Church," in the west end of the building.
It was altered days now from the time when they could call
Earls and Councillors to their bar to answer for their political
doings, as they did after "the Engagement."

The garrison was withdrawn from the Castle, as they called
the Palace now, in November 1659, the town being offered
the keeping of it if they would give a bond of £1000 to keep
it for the Parliament, an offer, however, which was declined;
but the use of a room or two "upon the west-quarter whair

---

* See Carlyle's *Letters and Speeches of Oliver Cromwell.*

the souldiers lay" was conceded for town and county business. Shortly after followed the Restoration, and the triumph of the " malignants" who had hitherto submitted, very much against their will, to the domination first of the thorough-going Presbyterians—swearing Covenants, and submitting to church discipline, which they detested—and next to the firm repressive rule of Cromwell. Shortly, too, commenced the attempt to force Episcopacy on an unwilling people, with General Thomas Dalyell to dragoon them into submission. An anecdote of Dalyell's earlier days occurs in the Council Minutes, and is worth repeating, as shewing the natural character of the man :—

1639, July 9. The quhilk day the Provost, Bailies, and Counsall, considering the great wrong dóne be Thomas Dalyell, younger, of Binns, to George Bell, Bailie, one the Magdalene day last was, in sending for him and wrongouslie challenging him for dismissing of Thomas Make out of waird ; and thairwith minasing and assaying to have bereft him of his lyfe ; Ordeines summondis to be raisit agains him for his compeirance befoir the Secrat Counsall, to answer for the foirsaid wrong.

The rejoicings of the hitherto repressed " Malignants" at the changed state of affairs were extreme, and one of the extremest cases of this occurred here in May 1661,* on the occasion of the anniversary of the Restoration, when they burnt the Covenant, which King and Courtiers all had formerly sworn to maintain. This act was long considered to be an opprobrium to the place, and the Council are found long after, in 1696, ordering search to be made in their minutes to see what part their predecessors had taken in the matter, and finding " nothing therein appointing the same to be done," declaring " that the Toun had noe hand in burning the Covenant, and any aspersion put upon the Toun thairanent to be false and calumnious." The following account of this affair is from a manuscript written about the time, in the possession of a gentleman in the Register House. Another account, not so complete, may be found in *Cruickshank's History of the Church of Scotland,* from which a few corrections have been adopted.

---

* A story appears in the *Mercurius Caledonius* Newspaper about this date to the effect that the swans, which had left the loch in disgust at Cromwell's garrison (who very possibly did not feed them in winter), returned to their old quarters at the Restoration !

After publick service the streets were filled with bonfires on both sides of the streets, that it was not without hazard to be among them. The Magistrates about four o'clock in the afternoon went to the Earle of Linlithgow's lodging, inviting his lordship to honour them with his presence at the solemnity of the day. The Magistrates were Andrew Glen provost, Robert Milne, Thomas Hart, George Bell, James Glen, baylies. The Earle of Linlithgow came with the Magistrates to the mercat place accompanied with many other gentlemen, where a table was covered with confections. They were met with the Curat of the place, Ramsay (now Bishop of Dunblane), who prayed and sang a psalm (O that prophane and ungodly villand that could worship God when about his wickedness), then eating some of the confections they threw the rest among the people; the fountain all this time running with French wine of several colours and Spanish wine, and continued two or three hours. His Lordship with the Magistrates and gentlemen drank the King and Queen's and all the Royal familie their healths, his Majesty's Commissioner the Earle of Middletoun,—breaking baskets of glasses. At the Mercat Cross was erected a crowne standing on an arch on four pillars. On the one side of the arch was placed a statue in form of an old hag having the Covenant in her hands with this superscription, A GLORIOUS REFORMATION; and on the other side of the arch was placed another statue in form of a Whigmuir having the Remonstrance in his hand with this superscription, NO ASSOCIATION WITH MALIGNANTS; and on the other side was drawn a Committee of Estates with this superscription, ANE ACT FOR DELIVERING THE KING; and on the left side was drawn a Commission of the Kirk with this superscription, ANE ACT OF THE WEST-KIRK; and on the top of the arch stood the Devil as ane angel with this label in his mouth, STAND TO THE CAUSE; and in the middle hang a table with this litany,

> From Covenanters with uplifted hands,
> From remonstrators with associate bands,
> From such committees as govern'd this nation,
> From kirk-commissions, and their protestation,
> *Good Lord deliver us.*

Over the pillar at the arch beneath the Covenant were drawn kirk-stools, rocks, and reels; and over the pillar beneath the Remonstrance were drawn beechen cogs and spoons; and on the back of the arch was drawn Rebellion in a religious habit with turned up eyes, in her right hand LEX REX, in her left a piece called THE CAUSES OF GOD'S WRATH; round about her was lying all Acts of Parliament, of Committees of Estates, of General Assemblies, and of the Commissioners of the Kirk, with their protestations and declarations during the 22 years Rebellion; above her was written this superscription, REBELLION IS AS THE SIN OF WITCHCRAFT. At the drinking his Majesties health fire was put to the frame, it turned it into ashes, and there appeared, suddenly, a table supported by two angels, and on the other side the dragon, the devil, that fought with Michael the archangel, with this inscription :—

> Great Britain's monarch on this day was born,
> And to his kingdoms happily restor'd :
> The queen's arriv'd, the mitre now is worn,
> Let us rejoice, this day is from the Lord.
> Fly hence, all traitors who did marr our peace ;
> Fly hence, schismatics who our church did rent ;
> Fly, covenanting, remonstrating race ;
> Let us rejoice that God this day hath sent.

The Magistrates then did accompany the Earle to the Palace where was erected a magnificent bonfire. The Earle drunk the King and Queen's good health, also, the Royal family's health. Thereafter the Magistrates made their procession through the streets.

Everybody did not rejoice, however, although most of the people kindled their bonfires. In 1663 the Council are found recommending the Bailies to "make enquiry of the diligence of the Session in finding out those who, out of contempt, did not attend church on the King's night," and in June 1664 they are found imposing a fine of five pounds each on those who did not kindle bonfires on the anniversary day. Episcopacy was again in the ascendant, and it was resolved to trample out all spirit of opposition to its establishment and continuance. The Session records are awanting from July 1660 till May 1673, but from that year a sample may be taken of much of what must have gone on before :—

1673, June 17. Alex. Wilson, mason, under Carribber, compeiring this day to answr for procuring baptisme to his child unwarrandably, confest he had procured baptizme to his child from a Minister of the Gospel, but refused to tell the minister's name, nor where it was done, nor when he was in the church on the Lord's day. The Session referred him to the Magistrates for making him lyable to the Law.

The town appears to have been very fortunate in its first-minister, Mr Alexander Seton, although he seems never to have been on good terms with the Council, and scarcely with any one, as according to his own account, scarcely any came to hear him preach. Possibly neither the Council nor the minister wished to harass their fellow-townsmen, and each blamed the other for the "irregularities" prevalent.* The Council on one occasion blame Seton as the principal cause of them all, as he, they said, "encouraged the phanaticks to continue the conventicles, by saying, 'poor people why sould they be hindered in preaching and praying whar they pleised !'" Shortly after he is found a little more diligent, and the following is one of his cases :—

1676, January 30. Archd. Henry represented in Session to be trafecting up and doun the burgh and paroch visiting and praying to sick persones dein, deiling damnation to them to their great astonishment and hazard and grief

---

* Seton was presented in 1665 by the Bishop of St. Andrews. He was a brother of Sir Walter Seton of Northbank, and was himself latterly proprietor of Hiltly—both places in the neighbourhood.

of their friends, is recommended to the Magistrates to oblidge him to be lyable to the Law.

The Council seem to have temporized as well as they could, but the fact of their remissness in enforcing the law in its stringency would not hide, so the Earl of Linlithgow appears in 1681 at the Council board with a commission requiring the Councillors to subscribe the Test on their knees—a bitter pill which they took four months to get over, some, including the Town-Clerk, demitting, "not having cleirnes." A worse dose still was in store for them, however, in a visit of a committee of Privy Council in 1683 to take the magistrates to task for their "neglect in punishing phanaticks." There is little in the Council minutes on the subject, only the Council could find no one at next election to act as Provost, and Lord Livingston was appointed to the office by the Privy Council. The records of the Kirk-Session show only a significant blank. The atrocities committed during the dismal reigns of Charles II. and his successors, were, however, rather witnessed than fully experienced by the people here, unless, indeed, the record of them be lost or purposely destroyed. One of the bailies of the burgh, who figures in the Session books as one of the "fanatics," by name William Higgins, came out after the Revolution as a minister of the church. The neighbourhood of Borrowstounness seems to have been more fertile in victims, one of whom was a servant girl, called Marion Harvey, who was hanged at Edinburgh for hearing Cargill, who frequently visited the neighbourhood, preach, and for holding intercourse with intercommuned persons.* In the excitement of religious controversy, a sect calling themselves "Sweet Singers" arose in Bo'ness, under the leadership of John Gibb, a sailor. They expected the immediate advent of the millennium. A body of them once set themselves down on the slopes of the Pentlands to witness the destruction of Edinburgh by fire from heaven. John is found by-and-bye cooling his brain in Linlithgow jail.

---

* Sir Robert Hamilton, the leader of the Covenanters at Bothwell-bridge, is said to have taken up his residence at Borrowstounness after the Revolution. This was for convenience of correspondence with the members of the United Societies, as the extreme covenanting party then termed themselves, resident in Holland or elsewhere abroad. He is said to have died and been buried in Borrowstounness.

Some incidental touches which bring the realities of history home, occur in the records, such as an order to the magistrates to secure riderless horses which had run off from the fight at Pentland. An order from Dalyell runs:—

——*th the 3d off May 1667*

Provoast
You shall Delyver the prisonners which is In your Custodie to the Laird off Hatton or any who Commands In His absence as Lykwayes the Amunitione—T. DALYELL.

And this is the receipt given to the magistrates:—

Receaivit be Archibald Douglas, Cliftonhaugh, Ryder in the Laird of Hatton his troup, at command of our Loutenant ffrom Robert Crawford and Umphra Welsh two of the baillies of Linlithgow by the above Comand the Magazine ffollowing viz. Threttie and two Muskets, two barrells of powder Mair ane other barrell with som powder in it, also four powder bags with some powder in the bags Mair ane barrell of Baall, with two hyds and thrie secks with Match Mair aucht prissoners I grant the Recept of the above written Magazin and prissoners be this present subscribit with my hand at Linlithgow the ffourth May 1667. There is two of the above written prissoners seik and not able to travell so the two is left in the prison of Linlithgow.—AR. DOUGLASSE.

From the Kirk-Session minutes we have, " June 1679, Inne regard there was no sermon in regard of His Majesties forces marching through the toun befoir Bothwel Bridge ffecht." Another notice of this same fight occurs in Kirkwood's amusing pamphlet, *The History of the Twenty-seven Gods of Linlithgow.* Though " exceeding loath to speak so of himself till he was forced to it for his own vindication," he thus narrates some of his own good deeds:—

Now how kind and familiar, not to say bountiful, Mr Kirkwood has been to Presbyterians in their lowest Condition, while lying in Prison, and in very great Straits, many in *Lithgow* can yet attest ; and Hundreds in that Country yet remember, what he did after that Fight at *Bothwell*, when about 1200 Prisoners, most of them naked, were carried through the town to *Edinburgh*, he pitying these poor distressed People, went to the Captain *Alexander Brown* of *Thornidike*, who commanded the Guards, being of his old Acquaintance and Condisciple, and got from him his Cane, as a token to the Souldiers, not to hinder him to do the Prisoners all the kindness he could ; for People were not easily permitted Access, some of the prisoners having made their Escape by means of those that went to them ; and there from Three in the Morning, till Ten in the Forenoon, he alone stood on the Flesh-market Wall, and gave in over it above 300 Suits of Cloaths, and exceeding much Meat and Drink, not without hazard of his Person, being often like to follow the Cord, with which he let down the Barrels to those Prisoners, of whom many thereafter came back and thanked him heartily, for the Favour he had done them."

The accession of James VII.,* more deeply immersed in the dream of divine right than even his father, brought no relief; and no elections of Town Council even were permitted in his reign, the magistrates being nominated by the Privy Council. It was not wonderful that the people got thoroughly tired of the Stuarts, and so thoroughly disgusted with their absurd pretensions as emphatically to declare that James, when he ran away, had not merely abdicated, but forfeited his claim to the crown. Claverhouse—the infamous cold-blooded persecutor of the lowland presbyterians, now Lord Dundee—the "bonnie Dundee" of Jacobite minstrelsy, was leader of the opposition to this finding, and the Convention of Estates which sat at Edinburgh in 1689 are found on the 19th of March ordering "that a Herauld be sent to the Lords Dundee Levingstowne and others with them at Lithgow or Stirling to returne to the meeting on twenty-four hours on payn of treason With indemnity what is done if they Lay down their armes Immediately." Farther on the macer reports "that he hade not mett with the Lord Dundee But he left a coppie at the house he was informed the Lord Dundee did lodge at Linlithgow." "Ere the King's crown goes down there are crowns to be broke," says Dundee in the ballad, so, in July following, he fell at Killiekrankie, opposing the Revolution. William and Mary were now on the throne, and the long fight against the establishment of arbitrary power was over. Even the Kirk was quiet over its divine rights, and those who were dissatisfied with the new settlement, formed at the one extreme the Scotch Episcopal Church, and at the other the United Societies men, now known as Cameronians and Reformed Presbyterians.

Kirkwood, who was appointed in room of David Skeoch (a schoolmaster removed in 1675 for attending conventicles), gives a curious satirical picture in his pamphlet, of some of the doings of the time. Amongst these he relates that at the Revolution the inhabitants assembled in arms at the Cross to the number of some hundreds, and sent orders to the two ministers to vacate their offices. It does not appear that this

---

* James VII., when Duke of York, paid the Town a visit in 1681, when he was entertained at great cost in the Town-house by the Magistrates. The expenses amounted to 1856 lib. 7s. 6d. Scots.

" rabbling of the curates" was effective here, but the second minister was shortly afterwards removed for refusing to pray for King William and Queen Mary.

The Presbyterians were in power once more, with Walter Stewart of Pardovan,* a young man, according to Kirkwood, hardly yet major, at their head as Provost; and poor Kirkwood was forced out of the school because he would not, he says, attend the Presbyterian meeting (still held, he says, in Stewart's kitchen), until he saw whether Presbytery or Episcopacy was to be established as the national church government. Kirkwood,† like his predecessor, Ninian Winzet, was clever, and fond of arguing a point, and so could not agree with men whom he too much despised. His book professes to be an account of the plea between himself and the Town Council, occasioned by their forcible ejection of himself from the school, and of his wife, Goletine van Beest, and his fine Dutch furniture from his dwelling-house. It would occupy too much space to follow all the law and lawless proceedings which occurred, but it may be mentioned that the affair was

---

* The site of the house in the town occupied by Stewart is still pointed out. The house itself was taken down ten years ago. An old lintel gives the date, 1596, and the initials of Robert Stewart and of Janet Forrest, the representative of Henry Forrest, the first provost, and through marriage with whom Stewart acquired the property. Ceilings do not seem to have been in use, as the joists and under surface of the floors above were, as well as the walls and under surface of the roof of the upper storey, found to be gaudily decorated with heraldic devices and scroll-work. A copy of this ceiling has been preserved in the *Transactions of the Society of Antiquaries.* Walter Stewart built another house, at the east end of the town, probably the one fronting the old tower, for a residence. Walter Stewart was a very zealous Presbyterian, and his book, known as *Pardovan's Collections,* is still an authority on the procedure in Church courts. He left his estate of Pardovan and his house here to the Glasgow Society for Propagating Christian Knowledge. Stewart belonged to the party opposed to the Union with England, and as a member of the Scotch Parliament, joined in protesting against that measure.

† He was editor or rather author of a revised edition of Despauter's Latin Grammar, which was used in the schools under the name of Kirkwood's Grammar, until displaced by Ruddimam's. When examined before the Commissioners of schools and colleges, after the Revolution, as to the best Latin Grammar for schools, he declined giving an opinion, having previously published one himself. Being then asked what he thought of Despauter, he said, that " if its superfluities were rescinded, the defects supplied, the intricacies cleared, the errors rectified, and the method amended, it might well pass for an excellent Grammar." He was appointed, a few days after, to perform this work.

eventually carried before the Lords of the Privy Council, and did not terminate till 1712, Kirkwood gaining all his pleas, and the Council very glad to get rid of proceedings which had "cost the town so much uneasiness and expenses." One of the most ridiculous proceedings of the Council is that which gave rise to the title of the tract :—

"The Town Council alleged Mr *Kirkwood* said, *They had done him Injustice.* did thence infer, that he was *a Reviler of the Gods of his People :* For this Crime they fyned him in 200 Merks.

"Now know that they were due him the equivalent sum and so easily paid that Debt.   *   *   *

"Was it not, think you a mighty lucky hit of Providence that the Town's Debt and Mr *Kirkwood's* Crime jumpt so nicely, that the very Thought of man cannot discern a Difference. But what if the Debt had been triple or quadruple more, than it was ? That says nothing, a Crime committed against the Gods, being of infinite extent can reach it, tho never so high."

"By *Gods* they here mean the 27 members of the Town Council, the Provost, Four Bailies, Dean of Gild, Treasurer, Twelve Councillors, Eight Deacons; so that the Websters, Sutors, Tailors, are Gods in *Lithgow*. . . . . At the reading of the Information, it was pretty warmly debated by persons of honour, whether it was GOD *Provost or Kirkwood.* A Reviler of the Gods of GOD'S People or the Provost's People, or Kirkwood's People. Some were for One, some for another, some for none of them, averring it was not good Grammar, considering the context of the Information, and that instead of *His* it should be *The ; a Reviler of the Gods of the People.* Others cry'd out, it was the hight of Blasphemy, to call any Webster or Tailor in the kingdom a God."

In Kirkwood's time the Burgh School employed three masters, and the school for long after maintained a considerable reputation. Amongst its notable pupils may be mentioned John, Earl of Stair, who boarded with Kirkwood, and Colonel Gardiner, who lived at Burnfoot, near Carriden, in his youth.

When Prince Charles passed through the town, in 1745, on his way to the south, he was entertained, and the Palace-well was set a-running with wine in honour of the occasion, by the lady in charge of the Palace, Mrs Glen Gordon. Provost Bucknay, who is said to have been a Jacobite, had so little faith in the success of the Rebellion, as it is called, that he, like most other Jacobites, took himself out of the way.

After the marchings of the Highlanders, and of their pursuers, and the accidental burning of the Palace, in which they were lodged, by Hawley's dragoons in 1746, on the day after their flight from Falkirk, there is nothing of historical interest requiring mention in connection with the place. Regarding the burning of the Palace a good story is told of Mrs Glen Gordon, the keeper. It is said that, observing the disorderly conduct of the soldiers, she went to remonstrate with their General, and to get his assistance to extinguish the fire which already threatened the house, but finding her remonstrances in vain, she took leave of him in these words—" a-weel, a-weel, I can rin fra fire as fast as ony General in the King's army " —alluding to Cope's defeat at Prestonpans, and to Hawley's own on the preceding day. It has been averred, too, that Hawley was in no way sorry to witness the destruction of this monument of the doomed race of the Stuarts.

The Palace has stood since then a roofless ruin, saved only by occasional repairs from crumbling into a mass of rubbish. It was at one time in contemplation to fit it up as a barrack for prisoners of war, but the notion was abandoned at the request of the late Lord-President Blair of the Court of Session, who had purchased the estate of Avontoun, and built a residence in the neighbourhood. Other proposals to convert the Palace into County Court-buildings, and into a supplementary Register House for Scotland, have since been abandoned, and the attention and expense which the Commissioners of Woods and Forests now bestow upon it, promise to preserve for a long time to come what Sir Walter Scott has justly characterised as " one of the most striking objects of antiquity which Scotland yet affords."

THE ROCK AND THE WEE PICKLE TOW.

CHAPTER VIII.

DECAY OF THE OLD BURGHAL SYSTEM; AND

OTHER MATTERS.

THE exclusive privilege of trading within certain districts, which the burghs possessed, seems to have existed pretty entire until the end of the seventeenth century. Under this state of affairs, Blackness, the port of the burgh, seems, latterly at least, to have been a flourishing little place.

Sir Robert Sibbald, in his History of the County, has given an account of it, as it was in his time :—

Sir Robert Drummond of Meidhope (who lived [till] after the restoration of Charles the II.) declared to several of the Gentrie his neighbours, that he remembered to have seen only one house where now Borrowstounness and the other towns now continued to Carriden now stand. I know in my time that they and the South Ferry had some 36 ships belonging to them, though in all that tract upon the south side of the Forth, there is no place for ships to lye at, but at Blackness. Their are many rich men merchants and masters of ships living there, and the cities of *Glasco*, *Stirlin* and *Linlithgow* had a great trade from thence with Holland, Bremen, Hamburgh, Queensburgh, and Dantzic, and furnished all the west country with goods they imported from these places, and then loaded outwards with the product of their own country.

The increasing population of the country seems to have demanded increased accommodation, and the large proprietors on the shores of the sea set themselves, for their own profit or convenience, to supply it. The burgh of Linlithgow was in a low pecuniary condition, arising from the many losses sustained during the contests already enumerated, and the community could not afford the outlay requisite to enable them to maintain the position of their port. The first encroachment of this kind which appears, is the erection, in 1615, of the lands of Grange into a barony with the privileges of a free port. This encroachment, which threatened the interests of the burgh, was the subject of a compromise between the proprietor, Sir John Hamilton of Beircroft, and the Council, in which the erection is acceded to by the burgh on condition that the burgesses of Linlithgow should have access to and use of the port free of toll or custom, and that, when any vessel arrived with merchandise, the goods should be offered to the Council and burgesses, at a price below which they should not subsequently be sold to any one else.

The next affair of the kind was the erection of Queensferry into a Royal Burgh in 1636. In this case, Linlithgow opposed the erection, and an arrangement was come to in 1641, whereby Queensferry agreed to pay 10 merks yearly to Linlithgow as a sort of rent for their customs; the burgesses and guild-brethren of Linlithgow were to have the same privileges in Queensferry as its own; and before any foreigner got liberty to sell his cargo, twenty-four hours' notice was to be given to Linlithgow.

A more formidable opponent than either of these shortly
appeared in "the village of Borrowstounness," which, in
October 1661, the Council received information that "Deuk
Hamilton" was trying to get "erected into a Burgh-Royal or
Burgh of Baronie, or of Regalitie." The opposition of the
Council, backed as they were by the Convention of Burghs,
was unavailing, as the Duke seems to have succeeded, in
1668, in getting his town erected into a Burgh of Regality.*
Burghs of Barony and of Regality were shortly after declared
by Parliament to be entitled to the same freedom of trade as
Burghs-Royal, and it does not appear that Linlithgow secured
any special privilege in Borrowstounness. This was not the
only contest that the Burgh had with their formidable
opponent, the Duke, the removal of the Custom-house to
Borrowstounness being the occasion of one; and the attempt
to levy customs at the fair, in accordance with the charter of
1601 which conferred a right to the customs of all fairs held
in the county, giving rise to another.† The Council repaired
or rebuilt their house in Blackness, and got the Custom-house
retransferred; they even offered the inducement of the
freedom of Linlithgow gratuitously to all masters of vessels
taking up their residence in Blackness; but all would not do,
the influence of the Duke prevailed, and the Custom-house
was again taken away, and what was worse, the trade
followed it. Many lamentations there are in the Minutes of
Council for many years after, over the "decay of trade:" the
trade of the "unfrie places," they say about this time, "far
exceeds that of Lithgow;" and in 1700, getting notice that
the Duke of Hamilton was seeking power to levy an impost
for building a harbour, they protest "that the building the
said harbour at Bo'nes should not prejudice the Towns herbour

---

* It was made a Burgh of Barony after the extinction of the heritable juris-
dictions. Its affairs are now managed by Town and Harbour Trustees under
a special Act.
† These attempts to uphold the "rights" of the burgh sometimes led to
serious consequences. For instance there is amongst the town's papers a
"Submission" as to the amount payable to the wife and relatives of a tacks-
man of the Customs in consequence of his maltreatment and slaughter while
attempting to uplift the petty customs at Queensferry fair on 25th July 1628.
The plea of slaughter was dismissed, as the man lived for some time after, but
the parties offending were amerced in £800, Scots.

at Blacknes." It was finally settled in 1713 that the Custom-house should remain at Bo'ness.

It has been the fate of Blackness to dwindle away into a mere sea-bathing village for the good folks of Linlithgow and Falkirk, the remains of its pier still bearing witness, however, to its having been something more. The Castle, which, from its command of the upper waters of the Firth of Forth, was wont to be esteemed as one of the "keys of the kingdom,"* has had its original flat roof covered over with a sloping slated one; and is now fitted up as a magazine for powder and stores.

The merchant trade, "whilk was our subsistence" the Council say on one occasion, having thus departed, the town to some extent decayed, and the inhabitants had to look about for other employment. Defoe, in the course of his tour some time after the Union, describes Linlithgow as "a pleasant, handsome, well built Town," and gives the following picture of what he saw :—

At *Lithgow* there is a very great Linnen Manufacture, as there is at *Glasgow;* and the Water of the Lough or Lake here, is esteem'd with the best in *Scotland* for Bleaching or Whitening of Linnen Cloth : so that a great deal of Linnen, made in other parts of the Country, is brought here either to be bleach'd or whiten'd. . . . .
The People look here as if they were busy, and had something to do ; whereas in most Towns we pass'd through they seemed as if they look'd disconsolate for want of Employment. The whole Green, fronting the Lough or Lake, was cover'd with Linnen-Cloth, it being the bleaching Season, and I believe, a Thousand Women and Children, and not less, tending and managing the bleaching Business.

In 1795 the writer of the old *Statistical Account* describes this trade as among the things that were, wool-combing and the preparation of leather, and shoemaking, being then, as the last is still, the principal manufactures of the place. He says that there were then 100 persons employed making shoes, and that the number of pairs made in a year was 24,000. The population, according to his own survey, in 1792–93, was in the town 2282, in the landward part of the parish 939.

* It is usually averred that Blackness, Stirling, Edinburgh, and Dumbarton castles, are kept up in terms of the Treaty of Union. "There is no stipulation in the Treaty of Union as to the maintenance of any fortresses. How the popular belief to the contrary arose, I cannot say, but it is universal, although quite groundless."—*Note from Mr Robertson.*

The census of 1871 shows 3689 in the town and 1864 in the landward part of the parish. Besides shoemaking, there is still some currying and tanning of leather, and making of glue, the only other manufactories in the immediate neighbourhood being a distillery, a soap-work, and two paper-mills.

Borrowstounness, which, up to 1780, had ranked as the third port in Scotland, decayed after this, its trade passing into other channels; but it has since revived to some extent in consequence of the erection of large iron-works in its neighbourhood; and the extension to it of railway communication has led to the active formation of better pier and dock accommodation.

Almond Iron-Works, about three miles west from Linlithgow, may also be mentioned in connection with the manufactures of the district. Linlithgow, however, although its geological position is on the out-crop of the coal measures, is likely to escape the smoke, if it cannot reap the benefit, of the closer neighbourhood of such works. So long ago as 1718 a search was made for coal in the Burgh-muir, a little to the east of the town, and probably beyond the out-crop of the coal, by "Daniel Peak, gentleman," who took a fifty-seven years' lease of it, and also erected a mill at the back sluice of St. Ninians' mill for refining metals, but, being unsuccessful, this lease was taken off his hands in 1725. It must have been near this where King James VI. erected his mills "for the stamping, melting, and fyning of the mettell of his Majesteis" mines at Hilderston (about four miles to the south of Linlithgow). Mr Robert Chambers relates in his sketch of *Tam o' the Cowgate,* more properly, Thomas Hamilton, the first Earl of Haddington,[*] who flourished in the reign of James VI., that "Having worked a silver mine in Linlithgowshire into something like a good character, he sold it to King James for £5000; and it is said that the poor monarch never made 5s. more by the concern, the vein being in reality exhausted." The ore is the ordinary galena or lead ore, and occurs in veins in the mountain limestone. A company recently formed to attempt to work the ore profitably, has had as little success as his majesty. Atkinson, who for some conducted the refining,

---

* See Chambers's *Pocket Miscellany,* vol. 1.

gives in his *Gold Discovery in Scotland,* the following " pre-scientific" account of the opening of the Hilderston mine :—

" Sir Bevis Bulmer sett doune in his booke, the manner how the rich silver Mynes at Hilderstone in Scotland were found ; and how they were lost, &c. After the full discovery thereof he rested not untill he named them, calling one pitt or shafte there, God's Blessing, &c.   .   .   .   .   .

" Now concerning the first finding thereof, Sir Bevis saith in his booke, that it wes found out by mere fortune or chance of a collier, by name Sandy Maund a Scotsman, as he sought about the skirts of those hills neere to the bourne or water of Hilderstone. And the Scotsman, by meanes of digging the ground, hitt upon the heavy peece of redd-mettle ; no man thereabout ever saw the like. It had descended from a vaine thereof, where it had engendered with the sparr stone in forraine provinces called by other travillers Cacilla. And he sought farther into the ground, and found a peece of brownish sparr-stone, and it was mossie. He broke it with his mattocke, and it was white, and glittered within like unto small copper-keese, which is to be found in many common free-stones. And he never dreamed of any silver to be in that stone, and he shewed it to some of his friends ; and they said, 'Where hadst thou it?' Quoth he, 'At the Silver bourne, under the hill called the Kern-Popple.' Whereupon a gent. of Lythcoo sent him to seek Sir Bevis Bulmer about Glen-goner water, promising that if Sir Bevis did not take up the matter his expenses would be paid.

" The greatest quantity of Silver that ever was gotten at God's Blessing, was raised and fined out of the red-mettle ; and the purest sort thereof then conteyned in it 24 ounce of fine silver upon every hundred weight ; vallewed at vj score pounds starling the ton. And much of the same redd-mettle, by the assay held twelve score pounds starling per ton weight. But when the same mines befell unto the King's Majesty to be superiour or governour thereof, then indeed it was not so rich in silver altogether. . . . Untill the same redd-mettle came unto 12 faddomes deepe, it remaned still good ; from thence into 30 fathome deepe it proved nought : the property thereof was quite changed miraculously in goodness, it was worth little or nothing ; and more, uppon an instant, after the Brunswicks [miners from Germany] entered, it was quite altered in quality, but not in colour, fashion and heavines."

In connection with the old privileges of burghs must be mentioned the custody of the standards for weights and measures. These, while yet the "Court of the Four Burghs" was in existence, were apportioned out among these four for safe keeping; and the other burghs were furnished by them with copies. This privilege was afterwards confirmed to Edinburgh, Stirling, Lanark, and Linlithgow, by various Acts of Parliament. The standard of the peck and firlot was committed to the keeping of Linlithgow. An attempt was made in 1707, immediately after the Union, to set aside this privilege, a number of brass bushels being sent to Scotland for distribution among the burghs. The town, however, with

Stirling and Lanark, opposed this innovation, and it was ultimately arranged that the whole were to be sent here, " each Burgh to get one and a set of small wooden ones for 30 lib."*

Occasion seems to have been taken of the visit of Charles I. to crave a boon, which appears in the shape of a charter (1633) extending the authority of the magistracy over all the highways, roads, and paths, for a mile round the burgh. The heavy losses sustained from Cromwell's operations here form the occasion for the granting of the next charters. In December 1651 the Council "supplicate the English for diminution of the cess for the armie" on account of losses, a note of which, both of the common-good and of the inhabitants, was given in to Colonel Lytcott, who promised to befriend them,—the total amount being £20,500, sterling. No relief, however, could be given without new orders from the Protector, and the Commander-in-Chief recommends the Council to confer with the county gentlemen to share with them. An abatement was given for one half-year at least in 1657, but there appears nothing more. By 1659 the town appears to be recovering its prosperity, as the Council are then found rebuilding their much-prized Cross Well (which had been injured or destroyed by the English), by public voluntary subscription, as before. When the Restoration came, and the town had testified its loyalty so signally, as has been related, and had the Earl of Linlithgow to back their representation, their application for some compensation for their losses met with more consideration, and the Council got a grant (1662) of double customs for nineteen years, and the privilege of holding an additional Fair on the 14th of February annually. A farther grant or charter was procured, empowering the Council to impose a tax of 20s. on every boll of malt, or of 2d. on every pint of ale brewed in the town.

By this dubious style of compensation, money sufficient was raised to build the present Town-house. This was done in a very handsome way, from a design by John Mylne, the King's Master-Mason, in 1668–70. The building, as already men-

---

* The Linlithgow wheat firlot contained 21¼ Scotch pints, the barley firlot 31 pints, three Scotch pounds of Water-of-Leith being the standard of the pint.

tioned, was flat-roofed and balustraded, and had an open balustraded double-staircase in front. It would appear, also, that a spire, such as was subsequently supplied, was no part of the original design, as the Council are found, in 1673, sending James Heyslope, wright, to Edinburgh, to procure a design for one, and considering, in 1678, the offer of the deacon of the wrights to mount it.

The only remaining charters or acts in favour of the burgh are those relating to the Customs levied at the bridge over the Avon, at Linlithgow-bridge, and at the other fords and bridges on the Avon from the west-bridge (about seven miles from Linlithgow), to the mouth of the river. Before the date of these acts or charters, it would appear that the burgh kept up, or professed to keep up, a bridge over the Avon, but that it was in a very lamentable condition before the Earl of Linlithgow advanced money about 1660 to build the present structure, in consideration of getting a lease of the Customs for nineteen years. This lease was renewed by the King in 1677 for other nineteen years, but was resigned to the burgh in 1681, and, in 1685, the extended privilege above mentioned was conferred, for all time coming, by Act of Parliament. The right to levy Bridge and Town Custom from the Edinburgh and Glasgow Railway Company was recently the subject of a long litigation. After having been affirmed in favour of the Burgh three several times in the Court of Session, the Case was at length given against the Burgh by the House of Lords, in a decision which ingeniously avoided consideration of the points of law raised in the Court below. The recent "Roads and Bridges Act" has now made these Customs of little value.

The Earls of Linlithgow, whose devotion to the Stuarts led to their being attainted for their complicity in the Jacobite rising of 1715, may thus be considered benefactors of the burgh. In the days when lairdships were more numerous than they are now, and such places as Linlithgow were small capitals where these lairds kept up their town-houses, in which they resided for a part at least of the year, both for the convenience of being near the schools with their families, and for the sake of society, the Earls of Linlithgow, whose country house was at Midhope, and whose town house was the Palace, of which they were keepers, would be the great men of the place.* It was doubtless out of compliment to the family that the old burgh tune—to which (but musical antiquaries must decide) the burghers may have marched to Flodden—received the name of "Lord Lithgow's March."† It was during this time that Earl George built, in 1688, the family burial-place attached to the choir of the church. The above-ground part of it was lately removed by the Heritors, and was a curious example of the architecture of a time when the ideas of the mediæval artists were lost. The same may be said of the Cross Well, which was not formerly raised on so high a pedestal, but would in all likelihood be set low enough to allow of dipping out of the lower troughs, and it must originally have more nearly resembled that in the Palace.

The popular motto of the burgh, which is displayed on the front-piece of the Cross Well—MY FRUIT IS FIDELITY TO GOD AND THE KING—like the supplement to the motto on the arms of Glasgow, "LET GLASGOW FLOURISH *by the preaching of the Word*"—is probably one found after the Reformation,

---

* They built a house at Midhope after the Restoration. Some stones from the old house of the Drummonds have been built into the walls. One of them bears the pious inscription in black letter, 𝕿angene bepres 𝕵esus—*touch not the thorns of Jesus.* Such inscriptions were common on houses of the time of James VI.

† Its other name, which is believed to be the old one, is "The rock and the wee pickle tow." It appears as the name of a Tune in Ramsay's *Tea-table Miscellany*, published 1724. In Herd's *Collection* (1776) there is a Song to the tune, by Alex. Ross, schoolmaster of Lochee, Forfarshire. The song is not worth repeating as a whole, but the first stanza is quaint enough :—

> There was an auld wife had a wee pickle tow,
> And she wa'd gae try the spinnin' o't ;
> She louted her doun, and her rock took a-lowe,
> And that was an ill beginnin' o't.
> She sat and she grat, and she flate, and she flang,
> She flew, and she blew, and she wriggled, and wrang,
> She chokit, and boakit, and cried—like to mang—
> Wae's me for the dreary beginnin' o't.

This has evidently been suggested by a verse in the ancient ballad, "The Wife of Auchtermuchty," well known in its modern dress of "John Grumlie." The verse runs :—The calvis and ky met in the lone,

> The man ran with ane rung to red ;
> Than thair cumis ane illwilly cow,
> And brodit his buttock quhill that it bled.
> Then hame ran to a rok of tow,
> And he sat down to 'say the spinning ;
> I trow he lowtit ow'r neir the low—
> Quoth he, "This wark has ill beginning."

without Heraldic authority or concurrence, and intended to supersede the old popish-looking one, COLLOCET IN CŒLIS NOS OMNES VIS MICHAELIS—*May the might of Michael establish us in the Heavens!* Possibly the Act of 1673 was aimed at such innovations. The Emblazonment furnished in that year by Sir Charles Araskine, Lyon King of Arms, (and which is still preserved in the Burgh Charter-chest), thus describes the

" Ensigns Armorial :—Azure, the figure of the Archangell Michaell with wings expanded treading on the bellie of a Serpent lying with its tail fesswayes in base, all argent, the head of which he is pearcing through with a Spear in his dexter hand, and grasping with his sinister, ane Inescutcheon charged with the Royall Armes of Scotland, The Motto being COLLOCET IN CŒLIS NOS OMNES VIS MICHAELIS. And upon the reverse of the seall of the said Burgh is insculped in a field or, a Greyhound bitch sable, chained to ane Oak tree within ane loch proper. Which armes above blazoned I heirby declare to have been and to be the true and unrepealable signes armoriall of the above-named Royall Burgh of Linlithgow, for ever."

Most of the old burghs had certain common lands attached to them, part of which was usually a common of which the burgesses were entitled to make free use. The Burgh-muir here was enclosed about the year 1675. The following abstract of the usual items of the debit side of the Treasurer's account about 1540, shews the value of the landed property, as well as the other sources of burgh revenue, at that time :—

	£	s	d
Balance in hand or outstanding from last year	56	9	0
Rents,—Lonyngs 40s, Flask and Leech-loch 59s, Burghlands 53s 4d, Masons Parks 25s, 7s 6d, 7s 6d, Flaskhill 18s, Bogside 53s 4d, Carmontlaws 29s, a Feu 6s, Shops, Cellars, Tavern and Volt, in the Tolbooth or Town-house, 68s.	18	6	8
Burgh Customs £15, 15s ; Blackness Customs 10s	16	5	0
Bell, and Street-sweepings	1	4	0
Entries of Burgesses	4	16	0
Procrases*	23	5	9
Churchyard dues	2	16	8
Legacies	1	7	0
Donations to "kyrk werk"	2	4	0
Prior of St. Andrews' dues to do.	3	6	8

The lands are all sold, but the old custom of inspecting the boundaries is still kept up. This "Riding the Marches" has

---

* This item in the accounts, supposed in Chapter V. to be the altar dues and fines of the trades, probably included these. The entry occurs once as " procrases and offerends of the kirk," and at another time as " procrsyis at the kyrkend." It appears again as " procuranis," and the word is probably a contraction or corruption of *procurationes.*

come, by long-continued use, to be held on the Tuesday in June which follows the second Thursday. When the incorporated trades and fraternities still retained their privileges, and riding in wheeled vehicles was scarcely known, the ceremony was picturesque, and even imposing. Each trade had its banner, and some of them a peculiar style of personal decoration, and there would sometimes be twelve different companies and three hundred riders. It has been popularly supposed that the keeping up of this ceremony is a condition of some of the old charters, and that the burgh would lose some of its rights should they suffer it to go down. This notion is possibly founded on a reference to it in the charter of 1593, which, amongst other things, confirms to the burgh their lands, "as they have enjoyed and perambulated them in time past." The earliest references in the Court-book to the custom occur in 1541 and 1542 :—

1541, Oct. 19. That all the common lands of the burgh mure and utheris, and all common passagis, als weill without the burgh as wyndis within the samyn, be vesitit seigne and considerit zeirlie, upon Pasche Tyisday, be the provost bailies consale and communitie, and reformit and mendit quhair need is.

1542, April 17. The Assys ordains the Provost and Bailies to sett ane day that the consale and hale communitie mycht pass abowt the comon lands and to sett merches as wss is of uther borrows.*

---

* The practice is still kept up in some other places—notably in Lanark, where the day is called THE LANIMER-DAY—a corruption possibly of Lanark-muir day ; and in Hawick, where the ceremony is called THE COMMON RIDING. At this latter part of the proceedings is the public singing of a song with the refrain—Terribus ye terrioden,

> Sons of heroes slain at Flodden,
> Imitating border bowmen,
> Aye defend your rights and common.

Our ancestors, who had no church organisation, and with whom every head of a family was its priest or pastor, seem to have held their religion somewhat lightly—not as explicit revelation of hard and fast matter of fact ; neither, apparently, had they any idea, when agreeing to profess the new religion, of submission to the rule of an authoritative priesthood. The church of course bided its time in the hope of securing authority over the rising generations. The new faith seems to have been held for long in much the same fashion as the old, as our ancestors continued to invoke the old Gods even until they lost sight of the meaning of the words in which they did so, and here are the good folks of Hawick invoking the help of Tyr and Odin to this day—*Tyr haebe us, yea Tyr, yea Odin*—that is, Tyr heave or uphold us, both Tyr and Odin. See Murray's *Dialects of the Southern Counties.* The music to which the song is sung seems to be that of an ancient battle hymn. The age of the Selkirk tune, to which the comparatively modern song of "The Sutors o' Selkirk" is sung, has not been ascertained.

The perambulation now consists in a visit to Linlithgow-bridge, where the Burgh Mill was situated, the limit of the jurisdiction to the west, and then to Blackness, where the magistrates hold a court on the Castlehill, calling their vassals before them (who, however, never appear), and appoint a Bailie for the port—a nearly nominal office now.*

The self-electing system, the introduction of which has been already traced, seems, so far as ascertained, to have prevailed, with little interruption, down to the passing of the Municipal Reform Act in the reign of William IV. Before the passing of the Parliamentary Reform Bill, the Town Councils chose the members of Parliament; Selkirk, Peebles, Lanark, and Linlithgow, latterly returning one member, and a "good correspondence" was kept up by the Councils on the subject of the elections. Bribery of Deacons and Councillors prevailed of course in all contested elections, and the bribery and management extended to the members of the incorporated trades, so as to influence them to return deacons who would vote as wished in the Council. One of these contests (1754), conducted here with much violence, led to a double election of council and magistrates, and an expensive law-suit between the parties to determine which was the Council—the result being that neither party were entitled to hold office.

"Among the useful institutions here, Dr Henry's library justly deserves to be named. That gentleman, well known to the world by his valuable history, having experienced the sweets of knowledge himself, benevolently wished others to share them. With that view, he bequeathed his books, under certain regulations, to the magistrates and town council, and ministers of the presbytery of Linlithgow, as the foundation of a larger collection. It is to be hoped, they will show themselves worthy of the trust, and promote a design of such general utility."

Dr Henry spent the last few years of his life at Millfield, near Polmont, about four miles west from Linlithgow. He died in 1790, and was buried in Polmont Churchyard, and

---

* About the middle of last century, when the Incorporations were still in their glory, the town abounded with the class of persons known as "characters," and there exists a curious little pamphlet, the work of some young men of the place, in the form of a play, entitled *The Marches-day, a Dramatic Entertainment of three Acts, as annually performed by the Originals at* ———, in which the peculiarities of the individuals—some of them till lately remembered—are happily hit off, and a racy though rough picture presented of some phases of the country-town life of the time.

the above notice is from the old *Statistical Account* (1795). Besides classical works, and the usual theological books found in a clergyman's library, there are the various historical and antiquarian works accumulated during the composition of his own History of Great Britain. From some ill-working provisions in the will, it is alleged, as to the management, Dr Dobie's anticipations have been sadly falsified. The remains of the library are now deposited in the Session-house of the Church, and Dr Henry's portrait, by Martin, an eminent portrait painter of his day, adorns the Council Chamber.*

The only public or prominent erections which have not come under notice in the course of the narrative, are the County Hall, the various dissenting Churches, the Poorhouse, and the Commercial Bank, a building in the Scotch Baronial style, which is said to stand on the site of what was of old the principal Inn of the place, and behind which still stands one of the old round Dove-cots of the fifteenth or sixteenth century.†

The County Hall is situated behind the Town-house, and though externally plain, the interior is handsome and convenient, and the large hall contains a fine portrait, by Raeburn, of General Sir John Hope, afterwards Earl of Hopetoun, who was second in command of the army in Spain under General Moore; another by Sir John Watson Gordon, of General Sir Alexander Hope, brother of the same Earl, who for eleven successive Parliaments was member for the county; and a third, by J. R. Swinton, of London, of the late Earl of Rosebery, for many years Lord-Lieutenant of the county. It was through the influence of his Lordship that the restoration of the "four orders" on the outer gateway of the palace was effected. The Hopetoun family when they purchased the estate of Abercorn acquired the then heritable office of Sheriff

---

* The books are under the charge of the Presbytery, in terms of an arrangement made with the Town Council in 1852. Many of the volumes had been destroyed when the Town-house (where they were then deposited) was burnt in 1847; but the Library had been closed for some years before that.

† The most recent addition to the historical mementoes of the place is one of the Russian guns from Bomarsund, presented by Government to the Council and inhabitants. It was (under the superintendence of Admiral Sir James Hope, of Carriden, who served in the Baltic fleet) mounted upon an oak carriage made after the model of those used in Bomarsund.

of the county, and since 1715 the Earls have generally been its Lord-Lieutenants. Charles, first Earl, appears in the Council Minutes directing that a Guard of thirty men should be kept in the Palace, and the Council are found supplicating him for 200 stand of arms, they having only 200 to supply the 400 "fencible men" in the town. Hopetoun House, about six miles from Linlithgow, near the old castle of Abercorn, was built about 1700 from a design by Sir William Bruce, the restorer of Holyrood, and the wings in front were added near the end of last century, under the direction of William Adam.

Of the dissenting churches, the oldest erection is the East United Presbyterian "Meeting-house," built in 1805, when the congregation changed their place of meeting, and is only remarkable as an advanced type of the churches of the Secession of 1733. The congregation originally met at Craigmailin, a few miles to the south. After the split of the Secession into the two parties of Burghers and Anti-Burghers, they adhered to the latter. The West United Presbyterian Congregation was formed in 1772, and adhered to the Burghers. The present Church, as also the Congregational Chapel, which accommodates a small body of Independents formed at the time the Haldanes commenced preaching, are recent erections. The Free Church, built after the Disruption, has been converted into a school for the landward part of the parish, and a new one with a handsome spire erected near it. The Poorhouse, which, under the new Poor Law, may be said to replace the old "Hospital" of the town, belongs to a combination of eight parishes, and was built to accommodate 270 paupers, but at present has only about 150 inmates.

Extensive repairs and alterations were made on the Church in 1812, when the choir and a portion of the nave were fitted up with pews and galleries in the usual style, and the open oak-timber roof of the wester half, and the ceiled one of the choir, were removed, the dividing arch of the nave taken down, and a new roof with plastered ceiling was placed over the whole. The light and elegant crown which adorned and relieved the heavy square tower was removed about 1821—

(leaving the outer battlement and the four balance turrets) —from an apprehension that it must otherwise fall. It has not since been restored, although designs were got at the time, either for finishing the tower in a plain way or for restoring the crown.* The incorporated trades, who, after the Reformation, had their dues to the altarages changed into the upholding of the church windows, claimed a sort of vested interest in the building, and the shoemakers held for a time the privilege of holding the annual meeting for the election of their deacon in the south transept, known as St. Katherine's aisle. The part occupied as the Parish Church has recently been cleared of whitewash and repaired, as well as furnished with a very fine Organ, built by Messrs Harrison & Harrison, of Durham. After the Reformation the burgh retained the appointment of the ministers, as well as the management of the churchyard. At first the parishes of Linlithgow, Kinneil, Carriden, and Binny, were attached to Linlithgow, which was a collegiate charge, with two ministers. Kinneil and Carriden got a minister between them in 1588; Carriden had a minister of its own in 1621; Borrowtounness was disjoined from Kinneil in 1649, and re-united after 1690. Binny does not appear to have ever had a minister for itself; and the second charge of Linlithgow was suppressed in 1744.† The burgh was deprived of the power to appoint the minister at the re-establishment of Episcopacy in the reign of Charles II., the advowson or patronage being then conferred upon the Archbishop of St. Andrews, although the parish was within the new bishopric of Edinburgh. At the abolition of Episcopacy in 1690 the patronage was retained by the Crown, and is now, by the recent Act, in the hands of the congregation.

It may also be mentioned, in conclusion, that in consequence of recent legislation, the title of the "twenty-seven Gods" is no longer applicable to the Town Council, the number of Councillors—including provost and three bailies—being now fifteen, who are also Commissioners under the "Lindsay Act,"

---

* One of the Engravings in the original edition of Sir Walter Scott's *Provincial Antiquities*, is a view of the Church, taken previous to the removal of its finishing ornament.

† Hew Scott's *Fasti Ecclesiæ Scoticanæ*.

which they have recently adopted, and under which the Municipal limits have been extended to the Parliamentary boundary; that, the police of the burgh being now conjoined with that of the county, the Council has now only one officer instead of the four—one to each bailie—that the Burgh maintained in its ancient state, before the days of the various "Boards," which now manage affairs that long ago came almost wholly under the control of the authorities of the Burgh.

Supposed Head of Edward I., from old debris in Palace.

H

APPENDIX.

SKETCH OF THE GEOLOGY OF LINLITHGOW,

By ARCHIBALD GEIKIE, Esq., F.R.S., Director of H.M. Geological
Survey for Scotland ; and now Murchison Professor of Geology
and Mineralogy in the University of Edinburgh.

THE town of Linlithgow stands on the eastern edge of a
great coal-field, which, stretching northward into Fife,
and west and southward across Stirling and Lanark,
occupies a large area of central Scotland. East from the
town the Lower Carboniferous strata appear and form the
undulating country as far as Edinburgh. They consist of a
series of sandstones and shales, often abounding with *stigmariæ, calamites, lepidodendra, sphenopteres,* and other
typical plants. On the shore at Queensferry, at Newton
three miles farther west, in the Railway cuttings at Craigton
and Winchburgh, and at Broadlaw near Binny Craig, there
are found a set of thin limestones and calcareous shales, containing in great numbers the remains of a minute bean-
shaped crustaceous animal called *cypris,* and also stems and
fronds of ferns. Other lower carboniferous plants are also of
frequent occurrence, in particular the *lepidostrobi,* or seed-
cones of a tall plant known as the *lepidodendron,* or *scaly-tree.*
The *cyprides* lived in fresh or brackish water, and the associated vegetable organisms were all denizens of the land.
Above these beds and nearer Linlithgow there occurs a great
series of sandstones and shales in frequent alternations. The
sandstones are well seen in Kincavel quarry, and the shales,

richly charged with *cyprides* and plants, attain a considerable thickness round the old mansion of Ochiltree. At the latter locality, too, and in many other parts of the eastern portion of Linlithgowshire, a seam of coal has been extensively worked. This is rather an unusual occurrence, a workable bed of coal being seldom seen in what is called the Lower Carboniferous group of strata. The present seam, with its equivalents in other districts, is perhaps the most ancient in Great Britain.

All the rocks here enumerated are more or less of a fresh-water origin: that is to say, when the sand and mud of which they are composed were deposited, Linlithgow was the site of a series of wide shallow lakes, or of a broad shoaling estuary, and once, at least, of a great marshy jungle, crowded with stigmariæ, reeds, and ferns. The strata undulate a good deal, but, on the whole, they dip towards the west, and sink below the town of Linlithgow, where they are succeeded by a higher, and of course newer, set of beds of a totally different character. These can be advantageously examined in a line of quarries commencing at Hillhouse, a mile and a half south of the town. They consist of a thick series of limestones, with interstratifications of sandstone and shale, and contain in great numbers the remains of the *encrinite* or stone-lily, at least three species of coral, along with shells of the genera *orthoceras, bellerophon, productus, spirifer,* &c. These are all evidently marine productions, and it is thus interesting to reflect upon the ancient changes of which these are the memorials; how, from the action of subterranean forces, lake, and marsh, and jungle, were all slowly submerged beneath the sea, and coral reefs began to form where once there bloomed a rank and luxuriant vegetation. Among these limestones thin seams of coal are sometimes met with. At the North-Mine lime quarry a layer of six or eight inches is seen resting on a fire-clay which represents the ancient soil, and surmounted by a sandstone full of the stems of plants, whence it would appear that occasionally the old freshwater conditions returned. These limestones belong to what is termed the mountain or carboniferous limestone group, and form the line of demarcation between the lower and upper carboniferous strata. Above them the upper or coal-bearing part of the system begins, extending north into the coal-field of Borrowstounness, and southwards into that of Bathgate. The space between these two localities is occupied by a series of hills sometimes over 1000 feet high, consisting for the most part of long parallel beds of greenstone dipping westwards. The coal-bearing strata are very thin among these hills, and the mineral has not been profitably nor extensively worked. The Borrowstounness colliery is one of the oldest in Scotland. There are seven or eight principal seams, one of them sometimes reaching a thickness of twelve feet, and also two seams of black-band ironstone. The Snab pit at Kinneil—one of the deepest in Scotland—was sunk to the enormous depth of nearly 1200 feet. Many of the shales in this coal-field contain well-preserved remains of coal-measure plants, also shells of the genera *posidonomya, lingula*, &c., and teeth of a large fish called *rhizodus*. Above all these fresh or brackish water beds, there occur two seams of marine limestone. The upper one has long been quarried at Bowden Hill, where the excavations have been carried on underneath the greenstone of the hill from side to side. The lower has been worked at Carriber.

Perhaps the most remarkable feature in the geology of Linlithgow is the number and variety of the igneous rocks. They are of three kinds. 1st, Beds of volcanic ash or *tufa* interstratified among the sandstones and shales. A good example is seen in the St. Magdalen's quarry, near the east end of the town, where the ash contains numerous fragments of coniferous wood. Other rocks of the same kind may be seen in different parts of the great range of limestone quarries, on the east side of Cocklerue hill, in Preston burn, below Carriden House, &c. 2nd, Beds of greenstone sometimes of great thickness and always conforming to the dip of the stratified rocks around them. Occasionally they are beautifully columnar as in the limestone quarries. All the more prominent hills in the neighbourhood belong to this series, so that this district, now so peaceful and luxuriant, must once have been the scene of long continued volcanic action, and where now we see woods and corn-fields there once rolled great sheets of molten lava, while the air around was darkened with showers of ashes. 3rd, Another form of igneous rock is that known as *trap dykes*, where melted matter has risen from below along the line of some fissure or dislocation. A well-marked example may be seen in the low ridge of Parkly Craigs, about a mile south of the town. This dyke can be traced at intervals as far as the Canal aqueduct at the Avon —a distance of fully four miles.

TABLE OF THE ROCKS IN THE NEIGHBOURHOOD OF LINLITHGOW : IN DESCENDING SERIES.

		Thickness.	Localities.
Lower group of Upper Carboniferous or Coal Measures.	Beds of Sandstone and Shale, with two marine limestones in their upper part and containing in their lower series interstratified seams of ironstone and coal, which form the Bo'ness and Bathgate coal-fields. Great sheets of greenstone and tufa are intercalated—more than . .	2000 feet	Bo'ness and Bathgate, with the intervening hills.
Middle Carboniferous or Mountain Limestone.	Beds of marine Limestone, with associated seams of sandstones, shale, and coal, greenstone, and tufa—average	100 feet	Hillhouse, Silvermine, and Bathgate.
Lower Carboniferous.	Sandstone and Shale, often in thick beds, abounding in plants, &c. The Sandstones are quarried for building purposes, and the Shales were formerly much used in making drains—perhaps not less than .	1000 feet	Kincavel, Ochiltree, and all the country immediately to the east of Linlithgow.
	COAL — averaging from a few inches to	6 feet	Houston, Hillend, Craigton.
	Thick strata of Sandstone and a little Shale—upwards of . . .	300 feet	Binny quarry, Railway cutting at Craigton, shore at Queensferry and Hopetoun.
	Bed of freshwater Limestone .	9 feet	Queensferry, Newton, Dechmont, &c.
	Sandstones and Shales	Thickness unknown, but very great.	District between Queensferry and Edinburgh.

The latest of the geological formations in the neighbourhood of Linlithgow is known as the *Drift*, and consists of a set of clays, gravels, and sands, scattered irregularly over the surface and plentifully interspersed with large rounded boulders. When this superficial matter is removed the harder rock below is generally found to be smooth and striated—the groovings pointing west and east or north-west and south-east, as in the sandstone quarry at Hillhouse, and on the limestone at the South-Mine quarry. It is believed that these scratched surfaces were produced by the grating of rock and sand frozen into icebergs that were drifting from the north-west when our country stood many hundred feet lower than it does at present.

SIR DAVID LINDESAY'S TALE.

From *Marmion.*

" Of all the palaces so fair,
    Built for the royal dwelling,
In Scotland, far beyond compare,
    Linlithgow is excelling ;
And in its park, in jovial June,
How sweet the merry linnet's tune,
    How blithe the blackbird's lay !
The wild-buck bells from ferny brake,
The coot dives merry on the lake,
The saddest heart might pleasure take
    To see all nature gay.
But June is to our Sovereign dear
The heaviest month of all the year :
Too well his cause of grief you know,
June saw his father's overthrow.
Woe to the traitors who could bring
The princely boy against his King !
Still in his conscience burns the sting.
In offices as strict as Lent,
King James's June is ever spent.
When last this ruthful month was come,
And in Linlithgow's holy dome
    The King, as wont, was praying ;
While, for his royal father's soul,
The chanters sung, the bells did toll,
    The Bishop mass was saying—

For now the year brought round again
The day the luckless king was slain—
   In Katharine's aisle the Monarch knelt,
   With sackcloth-shirt, and iron belt,
     And eyes with sorrow streaming;
   Around him in their stalls of state,
   The Thistle's Knight-Companions sate,
     Their banners o'er them beaming.
I too was there, and, sooth to tell,
Bedeafen'd with the jangling knell,
Was watching where the sunbeams fell,
    Through the stain'd casement gleaming;
But, while I marked what next befell,
    It seem'd as I were dreaming.
Stepp'd from the crowd a ghostly wight,
In azure gown, with cincture white;
His forehead bald, his head was bare,
Down hung at length his yellow hair.—
Now, mock me not, when, good my Lord,
I pledge to you my knightly word,
That, when I saw his placid grace,
His simple majesty of face,
His solemn bearing, and his pace
   So stately gliding on,—
Seem'd to me ne'er did limner paint
So just an image of the Saint,
Who propp'd the Virgin in her faint, —
   The loved Apostle John.
He stepp'd before the Monarch's chair,
And stood with rustic plainness there,
   And little reverence made;
Nor head, nor body, bow'd nor bent,
But on the desk his arm he leant,
   And words like these he said,
In a low voice, but never tone,
So thrill'd through vein, and nerve, and bone :—
'My mother sent me from afar,
Sir King, to warn thee not to war,—
Woe waits on thine array;
If war thou wilt, of woman fair,
Her witching wiles and wanton snare,
James Stuart, doubly warned, beware :
   God keep thee as he may!'—
     The wondering Monarch seem'd to seek
      For answer, and found none;
     And when he raised his head to speak,
      The monitor was gone.
The Marshall and myself had cast
To stop him as he outward pass'd;
But, lighter than the whirlwind's blast,
   He vanish'd from our eyes,
Like sunbeam on the billow cast,
   That glances but, and dies."

THE MARCHES DAY.

"OYEZ! OYEZ! OYEZ! The Burgesses, Craftsmen, and whole Inhabitants of the Royal Burgh of Linlithgow, are hereby Warned and Summoned to attend My Lord Provost, Bailies, and Council, at the ringing of the Bells, on Tuesday the —— day of June current, for the purpose of riding the Town's Marches and Liberties, according to the use and custom of this Ancient and Honourable Burgh-Royal,—and that in their best carriage and equipage, apparel and array; and also, to attend all diets of Court held and appointed upon that day by my Lord Provost and Bailies: and that under the penalty of One Hundred Pounds Scots each.—*God save the Queen and my Lord Provost.*"

The above is the form of summons, published by tuck of drum on the Friday preceding the important event, to the great delight of all the children of the place, who never fail to greet it with many hearty cheers. And many of the children of a larger growth listen and are glad, if less vociferous. The two or three hundredth whitewashing has done its best for the old houses, and they look, if not quite as good as new, cheerful in their old age. The ceremony, as already seen, is an old one, and it appears, in its origin, to have been something more than a mere ceremony. Since the dissolution of the Incorporations, it has been gradually dying away, and threatens at no distant period to become extinct,—but a short description of it as it was in its greater days may not be unacceptable. At present the day is usually opened by the arrival of some of the bands of music engaged for the occasion, but, in former days, when the town kept its piper, the first intimation used to be his clear lilt, with drum accompaniment, of "the Marches-day tune"—the Rock and the wee pickle tow. Horses arrived from the country and saddles were carried about, till near eleven o'clock, when the riders assembled at the houses of their deacons, where the deacons stood treat, until it was time for the several bodies to take their places on the sides of the wide street, east from the Cross. Issuing from the Council Chamber, the magistrates and other officials then proceed to make proclamation or "fence the marches" as it is called, first at the foot of the Cross-brae, a little to the west of the Cross Well, and then farther along the street, a little to the east of the Market-place, in the midst of the riders, in the following terms—the Town-Clerk reading and the Officer proclaiming:—

"I Defend and I Forbid in our Sovereign Lady's name, and in name of My Lord Provost and Bailies of the Royal Burgh of Linlithgow, That no person or persons presume nor take upon hand, under whatever colour or pretext, to trouble or molest the Magistrates and Burgesses in their peaceable riding of the town's Marches, under all highest pains and charges that after may follow.—*God save the Queen.*" *

---

* The following waggish variation occurs in *The Marches-Day:* "But in consideration of the many falls occasioned by mad horses, the Magistrates certify, That any accidents arising from the wanton disposition of these animals, shall be deemed involuntary. . . . And finally, the Magistrates, trusting to the unblemished character of the lieges, just hint at the mean practice of purloining bottles from the public dinners: But if, contrary to

The roll of the Deacons being then called, and each commanded to walk forward and show himself, my Lord Provost, Bailies, and Council, with the Town-Clerk, Fiscal, Schoolmaster, and other Burgh officials, preceded by their officers with halberds, and the flags of the Burgh, head the procession, which, according to the roll, should for the rest consist of the Incorporations of— 1. The Hammermen; 2. Tailors; 3. Baxters; 4. Cordiners; 5. Weavers; 6. Wrights; 7. Coopers; 8. Fleshers;* and of the Fraternities of—1. Gardeners; 2. Tanners; 3. Whipmen; 4. Skinners; 5. Curriers; 6. Dyers. The whole move off with banners flying, towards Linlithgow-Bridge, and shortly, after due refreshment, they march back through the Burgh, halting only to make proclamation as before at Bonnytoun Entry—in the midst of the old burgh lands. Here there is usually a break-up of the procession, and a scramble to the front for the honour of being first at Blackness—about four miles off. *Cockwell*, in his soliloquy, anticipates this part of the performance with evident gusto :—

"Weel faith this is ae day o' the year, on which ev'ry body pits on their best; and I'm resolv'd to show't awa as weel's I can. Whan I munt my horse, I'll gi' him the spur, gallop to the deec'ns, and daz the ane shall gang in the ranks before me; and as we gang east to the Cross, I'll glee frae this side to that side, kepp the lasses een, and smile i' their faces, gar my horse carry a high head, keep my taes into his side, and caper awa fu' bonnily :— and then down at Blackness—O I'll get rair fun !"

At Blackness the Magistrates hold a court "on the Green of Blackness, adjoining the site of St. Ninian's chapel, and a little to the south of the castle." The court is opened or "fenced" in the following terms :—

"I Defend and I Forbid in our Sovereign Lady's name, and in name of My Lord Provost and Bailies of the Royal Burgh of Linlithgow, That no person or persons trouble or molest this Court, nor one speak for another without leave first asked and then given, under all highest pains that after may follow.— *God save the Queen.*"

The proprietors of lands or tenements in Blackness holding in feu from the Burgh, are regularly called on to appear at these courts. The following is the list of the "Vassals," as they are termed :—

> The Right Hon. JOHN ADRIAN LOUIS, EARL OF HOPETOUN.
> ANDREW GILMOUR, Esq., Physician and Surgeon, Linlithgow.
> The Heirs of WILLIAM ALLAN, Farmer, Blackness.
> The Heirs of JOHN RITCHIE, Farmer, Blackness.
> HENRY CADELL, Esq., of Grange.
> ALEXANDER AITKEN, Esq., Falkirk.

---

imagination, any should be found amissing; in the foresaid names, I do declare, and hereby intimate, That the greatest pains shall be taken to bring the perpetrators to public disgrace."

* One of the Incorporations became extinct in 1638—that of the Walkers (Fullers or Cloth-walkers). This appears to have been a flourishing trade here as far back as 1540. A place in the neighbourhood is still called Waukmilton, and a part of the loch at the Deuk's Entry bears the name of the pany or pandy—a place for steeping cloth.

A Bailie for the port is then elected in open court—a singularly preserved remnant of the old open system. The Bailie's real duties now are to keep a good bottle in store for the Marches-day ! Returning to Linlithgow, the procession is re-formed at the east end of the town, and after riding round the Cross Well, the riders rank up on the sides of the street as before ; the magistrates and officials gallop through the midst, and a loud hurrah terminates the ceremony. The proceedings of the day are usually wound up with a dinner. When each incorporation had its own dinner, and manners were somewhat rougher, talk would be of "former days, similar to this, on which bailies were unhors'd, standards broke, their bearers thrown in the mire ; how the blood stream'd alternately from the sides of wayward horses, and the skulls of wayward riders ; how magistrates were assaulted, counsellors batter'd, and deacons trampled under foot."

The Blackness Bailie is usually called "Baron Bailie," in accordance with a popular but incorrect usage which has latterly become common, of so designating Bailies not Magistrates of Royal Burghs, or, as in this case, supposed not to be so. Blackness was never erected into a Barony, but was virtually part of the Burgh of Linlithgow. The distance of Blackness from the main part of the Burgh would necessitate the appointment of a resident Bailie, who was chosen annually by the burgesses in the same way as the other magistrates.

THE OLD HOSPITAL.

This institution, which appears to have been either an alms-house or a leper-house, or both, is chiefly interesting on account of the confused notices we have regarding it. The popular idea is, that it was, in the crusading times or before them, a "hospice" for the entertainment of pilgrims bound for the Holy Land ; and this idea has been supported by the name of "the Pilgrims' hill," long applied to the part of the road leading over the slope to the east of the supposed site of the hospital. The name of "Pilgrims' hill," however, never appears in any old writing, so that it is not known when it arose. An alms-house seems to have existed at the time of and for a century after the Reformation, until abandoned as useless. The charter of James VI. (1591) confirming the appropriation of the annual-rents of the altarages, bears that these are to be applied to support "a reader" in the church, and the "poor of the hospital." It appears, further, that the hospital at this time, and for some time previous, was situated in the Kirkgate. In an entry in the Town Council minutes, in 1637, the Council dispose of an old place in the Low-port, "whilk was of old the townes almous-house now demolischit." The lands of "St. Magdalen's Hospital" are said by Chalmers to have been alienated by the then preceptor to Sir James Hamilton of Finnart, in 1526, and it is supposed that this was the establishment under the charge of the Burgh prior to that time. The only notices regarding it previous to 1526, are,—the order of Edward III. appointing a preceptor in 1335, in which it is called simply "the Hospital of Linlithgow;" one in 1426, in which James I. appoints a preceptor (according to Spottiswoode) to "St. Mary Magdalen's Hospital;" one in 1448 amongst the "obits" or notes of legacies, in one of which twelve pence are left to the almes-house, and twelve pence to the leper-house of the burgh; and a fourth one (1496) in the Royal Treasurer's accounts, being a donation of twelve pence "to the seik folk at the town end of Linlithquho," that is, to the lepers. The assertions that the house at one time was an establishment of the Lazarite friars, and that it was not an almes-house, but an hospitium or hostelry erected by the magistrates in the time of James I., seem both groundless. It may be added that St. Magdalen's chapel, at least, stood near St. Magdalen's village; and that St. Magdalen's Cross, at the ancient market-place (place for holding fairs probably), stood where St. Magdalen distillery now stands.

ANTIQUITIES, &c., IN COUNCIL CHAMBER.

1. Set of Brass or Bronze Old Scotch Liquid Measures. The Burgh of Stirling had the custody of the Standards of Liquid Measure, and issued authorised copies to the other burghs. The set here bears the Arms of Stirling.
2. Wrought Copper Jug with Brass rim, bearing the inscription :—"This Jug Contains the Exact Quantity of the Stirling Jug and was adjusted at Stirling on the 2d day of Nov 1791 years In Presence of Henry Jaffray Esq Provost of Stirling and James Andrew Esq Provost of Linlithgow Conform to Act of Parliament James VIth 19 of Feby 1618"
3. The Branding Irons for the Firlot, the Standard of which Linlithgow was custodier of. The Firlot itself was destroyed in the fire which consumed the Town House in 1847. The copy of the Ellwand from Edinburgh was also burnt at the same time.
4. Three Brass or Bronze Bushel Measures. After the Union in 1707 an attempt was made to introduce an Imperial Standard of Weights and Measures. These Bushel Measures were intended to have been sent to each of the burghs, but the burghs which had formerly had the privilege or dignity of being custodiers of the Standards held out, and the copies of the Imperial Standards were sent to the respective burghs, from which all others were supplied. These three have been left over of the entire stock.
5. Large Weights of same issue.
6. Pile of Small Weights of same issue, Avoirdupois.
7. Nest of Small Weights of same issue, Old Scotch Weight.
8. Dutch Stone of same issue. These four lots have, besides the Imperial Stamps, the Stamp LK for Lanark, from which they have been procured.
9. Wine Gallon Measure of same issue.

10. Ale Gallon Measure, and two Smaller Measures of same issue.
11. The large Burgh Seal.
12. Hand of the old Town Clock.
13. Weather-cock of the old Steeple—burnt down in 1847.
14. Sword found near Linlithgow-Bridge in a grave on the battle-field there. The battle was between the Douglas faction and those led by the Earl of Lennox, for possession of the King, James V., who was then a minor. The battle resulted in the victory of the Douglases, and Lennox was slain there. The sword bears the motto PONO LEGES VIRTUTE—*I maintain the laws by valour*, on one side of the blade.

In the Council Chamber there is, also, a fine Portrait of Dr Henry, the historian, who left his Library to the Burgh and Presbytery of Linlithgow—the painting is by Martin, an eminent Scottish portrait painter of his day;

A Drawing of the Crown which adorned the Church Steeple, furnished by Mr Milne, of London, the lineal representative of the architect of the Town House; and

A Photograph of a proposed renovation of the Interior of the Church, by the late Mr Matheson.

Head, from old debris in Palace.

INDEX.

G. WALDIE,
PRINTER,
61 HIGH STREET,
LINLITHGOW.